T0330553

*Routledge Revivals*

# Unemployment Relief in Great Britain

Originally published in 1924, *Unemployment Relief in Great Britain* takes up the history of unemployment relief in Great Britain, focusing on the after effects of the post-war period and the Great Depression. Primarily, the book provides a detailed study of England's experience with compulsory unemployment insurance and public employment exchanges. The book provides an intriguing study that will appeal to sociologists and historians alike, adeptly weaving practical aspects of the insurance acts, and the administration of employment exchanges.

# Unemployment Relief in Great Britain

## A Study in State Socialism

Felix Morley

Routledge
Taylor & Francis Group

First published in 1924
by George Routledge & Sons, LTD.

This edition first published in 2018 by Routledge
2 Park Square, Milton Park, Abingdon, Oxon, OX14 4RN
and by Routledge
711 Third Avenue, New York, NY 10017

*Routledge is an imprint of the Taylor & Francis Group, an informa business*

© 1924 Felix Morley

**Publisher's Note**
The publisher has gone to great lengths to ensure the quality of this reprint but points out that some imperfections in the original copies may be apparent.

**Disclaimer**
The publisher has made every effort to trace copyright holders and welcomes correspondence from those they have been unable to contact.

A Library of Congress record exists under LCCN: 25001970

ISBN 13: 978-0-367-17952-6 (hbk)
ISBN 13: 978-0-429-05862-2 (ebk)

STUDIES IN ECONOMICS AND POLITICAL SCIENCE

*Edited by*

THE DIRECTOR OF THE LONDON SCHOOL OF ECONOMICS AND
POLITICAL SCIENCE

No. 77 in the series of Monographs by writers connected with
the London School of Economics and Political Science

UNEMPLOYMENT RELIEF IN GREAT BRITAIN

# UNEMPLOYMENT RELIEF IN GREAT BRITAIN

*A Study in State Socialism*

BY

## FELIX MORLEY
*Fellow of the Economic Society (England)*

LONDON

GEORGE ROUTLEDGE & SONS, LTD.

BROADWAY HOUSE: 68-74, CARTER LANE, E. C.

1924

**The Riverside Press**

CAMBRIDGE · MASSACHUSETTS

TO

THE PERSONNEL OF THE

BRITISH EMPLOYMENT EXCHANGES

IN TOKEN OF THEIR UNTIRING SERVICES TO

THEIR COUNTRY AND TO HUMANITY

THIS BOOK IS DEDICATED

# PREFACE

THIS series of books owes its existence to the generosity of Messrs. Hart, Schaffner & Marx, of Chicago, who have shown a special interest in trying to draw the attention of American youth to the study of economic and commercial subjects. For this purpose they have delegated to the undersigned committee the task of selecting or approving of topics, making announcements, and awarding prizes annually for those who wish to compete.

For the year 1924 there were offered:

In Class A, which included any American without restriction, a first prize of $1000, and a second prize of $500.

In Class B, which included any who were at the time undergraduates of an American college, a first prize of $300, and a second prize of $200.

Any essay submitted in Class B, if deemed of sufficient merit, could receive a prize in Class A.

The present volume, submitted in Class A, was awarded the second prize in that Class.

J. LAURENCE LAUGHLIN, *Chairman*
*University of Chicago*

J. B. CLARK
*Columbia University*

EDWIN F. GAY
*Harvard University*

THEODORE E. BURTON
*Washington, D.C.*

WESLEY C. MITCHELL
*Columbia University*

# AUTHOR'S PREFACE

"WHEN Americans ask me what the British Labor Party will do if it remains in power," observes an English visitor to the United States, "I tell them that a task certain to absorb the energies of its wisest leaders for several years will be defeating the effort of the old parties to turn Great Britain into a Socialist State."

Except incidentally this study has nothing to do with the British Labor Party, and nothing to say regarding Socialist doctrine, whether of the Guild, Collectivist, or Coöperative variety. But with the kernel of truth which lurks behind the above paradox, it is necessarily concerned. A fault which no orthodox economist has ever perpetrated is undue detachment from the dominant social philosophy of his time. The student who tries to explain the British system of unemployment relief will build without foundations if concentration on superficial characteristics of the program excludes consideration of the tendencies and theories on which that program rests. Therefore, it may be well to observe in advance that the present system of unemployment relief in Great Britain is an expression of State Socialism, thinly — if at all — disguised. The system with which an increasing number would replace present method is, by contrast, based on a very different and antagonistic social philosophy. Its proponents favor a progressive retrenchment of State-operated unemployment insurance and its progressive replacement with unemployment insurance by industry. We shall call the philosophy underlying this argument (in order to avoid an embarrassing definition at the outset) by that pleasingly vague word, "individualism."

At bottom, it is the present conflict between the theories of paternalism and individualism which makes the story of unemployment relief in Great Britain of much more than parochial or professional interest. And for the discerning observer of social tendencies this interest will be heightened by the fact that the conflict follows no party lines. Many Socialists as well as "captains of industry" urge an individualistic policy. Many who are most fretful over the growth of Labor's political strength stand on the same ground with spokesmen of that party in insisting that the paternalistic methods now in force be strengthened rather than abandoned. On one point only are both sides in full agreement: that communities, the very foundations of which are periodically menaced by the unemployment problem, and which fail to exert every possible effort to cope with that problem, are derelict in one of the most urgent duties of civilization.

The post-war depression in Great Britain has had one virtue. It has subjected the accepted practice of unemployment relief to an acid test which has rendered every defect distinct. An inevitable shortcoming of the few comprehensive studies of the British system undertaken prior to the depression period is that they failed to estimate at true importance weaknesses which were concealed prior to the time of test. Writing when these weaknesses had become apparent to every close observer, I have had an advantage over my predecessors. And believing that the successful system of unemployment relief must be buoyant enough to outride depressions even as drastic as that of the post-war period, I have made no attempt to excuse the shortcomings of the British system by overemphasizing the magnitude of the storm. On the other hand, it should be stressed that features which have survived the depression period in good shape are ones which may be regarded as having passed a test as severe as any which is likely to recur.

The reader who seeks a clear-cut moral in this chronicle of British experimentation should note at the outset the sequence which the theory of unemployment relief has followed in Great Britain. There is first the attempt through Local Government; then the attempt through National

Government; now (pending the development of better international organization) the theory that through Industrial Self-Government is the best method of approach. The first of these policies has long been looked upon as an inadequate makeshift. So far as State-operated unemployment insurance goes, the second method has failed, and the failure is doubly unfortunate in that it has obscured the promise of the National Employment Exchange system in its vital function of bringing order and method into the business of employment. Ground which the State has clearly won in the battle against disorganization must be held. Ground on which it has failed had better be abandoned. Insurance by industry is, even as a theory, in its infancy, but far greater promise is contained therein than in the bureaucratic methods of State-operated unemployment insurance which have been found wanting in the time of test.

Control in industry is flexible; control in bureaucracy is rigid. Industry can adapt itself to altering conditions and quickly shape new courses when they are necessary. The State has not the power to vary its unemployment insurance program as swiftly as the facts of economic life demand. Each industry knows the needs and conditions of its particular field. The State must treat all alike, opposing flat conformity to that diversification and initiative from which springs progress.

For an instrumentality such as the Employment Exchanges, where operation properly remains much the same from year to year, the State (assuming the fundamental decency of a Civil Service above politics) is the ideal agency to command. To operate social machinery as delicate and variable as unemployment insurance, on the contrary, the State is not fitted — not in its present form at any rate. Here, rather, is a function for coöperative industry, one of the many to which Joint Industrial Councils may devote their attention for the good of all.

For all the mistakes and defects in the British system of unemployment relief, it holds a position years ahead of that of countries, like the United States, where it has been possible to let undiscriminating *laissez-faire* be the dominant thought in confronting the problem of unemployment. Yet one great advantage America has gained by her indifference, even if it be purely negative in type. It is scarcely conceivable that any system of State-operated unemployment insurance will be attempted in the United States. Were the warning of unfortunate example necessary to prevent such a development, Great Britain has provided it, as the ensuing pages will point out. In the United States progress will come more naturally from the bottom — in the integration and linking-up by industries of such schemes of company and trade union unemployment insurance (that of the Amalgamated Garment Workers, for instance) as are already in operation. While pitiably slow, this method is secure. But the refusal of so many American employers to see in trade-unionism anything but an instrument of obstruction indicates that it will be long ere unemployment insurance in the United States becomes an important factor for social benefit. And since the virtual destruction of the war-time Federal Employment Service by Congressional action in 1919, the necessary basis for a balanced program of unemployment insurance has been lacking — the machinery for adequate test of unemployment is not there. To students of the problem it is some comfort that the United States Employment Service still remains as a skeleton organization, expandable in time of need.

At present American economic thought is more concerned with preventing unemployment than with relieving it. The trend has much to be said for it, as well as being entirely natural in a country individualistic in philosophy and economically independent. Yet it requires no prophetic mantle to maintain that neither experiments in the control of currency and credit, nor any other device for diminishing violent oscillations in the trade cycle will indefinitely postpone the advent of depressions with their grim train of social evils. No effort to avert unemployment is a wasted effort, and it is probable that Great Britain has overemphasized remedial as opposed to preventive measures. America, on the other hand, continues to maintain her traditional indifference to the problem of unemployment relief. The time will come when this neglect will be regretted.

This book has only indirect concern with theories of unemployment prevention, whether by artificial stabilization of prices, more equitable distribution of national income, or other schemes. Its major purpose is to be of some assistance in forwarding the rational relief of that unemployment which will continue in varying degree regardless of all preventive panaceas. There seems no better way to serve this purpose than by relating in critical manner what has been done for unemployment relief in Great Britain, the nation which above any in the world has concentrated on this problem. The story is told and the lessons inescapable from that story are drawn.

There are, of course, omissions which considerations of space and unity of treatment have rendered unavoidable, but it is believed that they are all minor in character. Because they have been stereotyped in nature and purely emergency in design, discussion of local and national relief works during the depression period scarcely extends beyond the bare summary given in Appendix VI. Special encouragement to emigration is not touched upon because, from a national viewpoint, it dodges without in any way confronting the unemployment problem. A more debatable omission is the failure to give more than a brief explanation to the interesting Export Credits and Trade Facilities Schemes set in operation by the Government in 1920 and 1921 respectively. They are not discussed at length, however, partly because they are temporary in character; partly because they are too experimental to warrant the considered judgment which can be passed on the major features of the system; and partly because they are measures aimed rather at stimulating the revival of industry than at relieving unemployment. The distinction may seem somewhat arbitrary, but it is there. Not emergency measures to lessen the surplus unemployment of a depression, but the minimum program for the relief of unemployment in good times as well as bad, is the subject of this study. It is an examination of principles rather than a catalogue of hastily improvised remedies.

With these qualifications it will be found that this book relates, as simply as is compatible with thoroughness, the story of unemployment relief in Great Britain from its inception as a settled responsibility of the modern State down to the beginning of 1924, at which time the turning-point in the great post-war depression in that country was definitely past. It was begun as an approved graduate thesis for the London School of Economics, and in addition to research conducted in different parts of England, a three months' inquiry into post-war unemployment relief in Germany, and certain observations made while attached to the Federal Employment Service of the United States Department of Labor, have been drawn upon by the author.

In particular, thanks are due to Sir William Beveridge, philosopher and guide for all students of unemployment; to Professor Edwin Cannan, who by his keen yet kindly criticism facilitated the difficult initial stages of the work; to Commander J. B. Adams and many other Civil Servants in the Ministry of Labor who always showed unfailing kindness and patience in making plain the operation of the British system of unemployment relief. For no less important assistance in making this study feasible, a debt of gratitude is owing to the Trustees of the Rhodes Scholarships.

To the Warden of Toynbee Hall and to Mr. H. W. Massingham, late Editor of the *Nation and Athenæum*, thanks are also due for permitting the republication of material originally prepared for their purposes.

FELIX MORLEY

*May*, 1924

# CONTENTS

# LIST OF TABLES AND CHARTS

# UNEMPLOYMENT RELIEF IN GREAT BRITAIN

# UNEMPLOYMENT RELIEF IN GREAT BRITAIN

∵

## CHAPTER I

### THE ORIGIN OF THE EMPLOYMENT EXCHANGE SYSTEM

THE establishment of a national system of Employment Exchanges in Great Britain has been no matter of mushroom growth. Such a development does not come in a Democracy until the public conscience and the public intellect alike have realized the advisability of assistance beyond the prevention of actual starvation to the able-bodied worker unemployed through no fault of his own.

It is not proposed to repeat the work of others in tracing the slow series of steps during the past half-century whereby effort has been made to separate the treatment of unemployment from the relief of pauperism. Nevertheless, a review of the more important landmarks leading to the present program is advisable. Among other reasons, because it will show that endeavor to withdraw as large a proportion of unemployed workers as possible from the demoralization of Poor Law and charitable relief has been a constant policy behind the development of State-operated Employment Exchanges and Unemployment Insurance. One obvious standard of the efficacy of the present system of unemployment relief is, therefore, its success in keeping the ordinary unemployed worker from drifting to the last resource of the degraded — Poor Law relief.

Between 1886, the date of the Chamberlain Circular to municipal authorities advocating local relief works for the "respectable unemployed," and 1909, when the Labor Exchanges Act was passed, the National Government followed a consistent, if negligent, policy of encouraging local relief works of various types to bridge depression periods for those unemployed "who do not ordinarily seek parish relief."[1] In the prosecution of this policy, however, the Central Government took no responsibility, offered little assistance, and (being itself in ignorance of how to attack the problem) gave none but the most general advice. The result was as might have been foreseen. In the absence of any coördinating authority and any machinery for the intelligent selection of those to be given employment, the experiments of the various local authorities soon fell victim to all the dangers which beset relief works viewed as relief work *per se*. Only the most ordinary type of unskilled work was attempted; each job undertaken was regarded as being as much task-work as the road-mending of convict labor; there was no attempt to make the work economically self-supporting. The extreme form of degeneration to which this ill-judged program was always liable was seen in the case of a London Borough Council which as late as 1904 for some months discontinued the use of its street-cleaning machinery in order to put unemployed to work sweeping the streets by hand.[2]

## THE UNEMPLOYED WORKMEN ACT

With each successive cyclical depression the futility of such a program of unemployment relief became more marked. Nevertheless, the effort to solve the problem by relief works organized by local authorities was not

[1] The circular to municipal authorities was reissued in much the same form during the depressions of 1892 and 1904.

[2] Beveridge: *Unemployment*, p. 157. In the United States such tactics are still met with. During the depression of 1921, the Mayor of Sioux Falls, South Dakota, "substituted hand digging for power in some sewer construction and water supply work." (Klein: *The Burden of Unemployment, 1923*, p. 76.)

only maintained long after its fruitlessness was generally recognized, but was even given a new lease of life by the Unemployed Workmen Act of 1905, hurried into being as a result of the trade depression of 1904. The primary aim of this Act, as Sir William Beveridge has pointed out, "was not to do any new thing, but to do slightly better what had been done before." [1] The idea of emergency relief works under municipal control, supplemented, it is true, by some assistance towards emigration and by a few farm colonies and other specialized training schemes, was retained as the only constructive assistance Society could offer the involuntarily unemployed aside from the Poor Law and privately organized charity. Consequently, this effort to disentangle temporary from chronic unemployment, to dissociate unemployment relief from Poor Law relief, failed just as dismally as had its predecessors. The elementary lesson that effective treatment of the unemployment problem is utterly beyond the power of local government had not been learned.

The program of minor relief works as conducted by the municipalities, generally improperly planned, launched at short notice and limited to odds and ends of unskilled work on trivial projects, was, of course, foredoomed. It has been asserted with some reason that relief schemes of this nature are of little more value to the community and little less demoralizing to those "relieved" than is an outright system of doles. Those who proffer the work do not expect it to be as economical as private enterprise, and those who carry it out do not expect to receive any more training or benefit therefrom than if they were ordered to dig holes and fill them up again in return for bread and shelter. The failure of relief work of this type is proved beyond doubt. And it is only natural, though none the less unfortunate, that the experience of a generation of such failure in England succeeded in stamping the very name "Relief Work" with opprobrium and

[1] *Unemployment,* p. 165.

helped to check development on novel and less restricted lines during the post-war depression.[1]

The Unemployed Workmen Act of 1905, however, while failing to solve the vexed problem of effective relief work for the unemployed, did prove of very considerable value in pointing the way towards the next important step — the establishment of a national system of Employment Exchanges. The Act established, in every municipality with a population of at least fifty thousand, a Distress Committee composed of officers of local government and local relief workers, on which was laid the statutory obligation to acquaint itself with conditions of labor in the area of jurisdiction. These Committees received applications from unemployed workers, and were supposed to investigate every application on its merits. Wherever a case was found to be "capable of more suitable treatment under this Act than under the Poor Law," special assistance, financed in the main from local taxation, might be provided, whether in the form of emigration or domestic migration assistance or in the provision of temporary relief work in the locality.

To facilitate the operation of this program, the Act instructed the various counties to establish Employment Exchanges[2] wherever Distress Committees were themselves not fulfilling that function. It was recognized at the time that a prerequisite for the success of the Act was a network of Employment Exchanges covering the entire Kingdom, but, owing to the mistake of treating a national problem from a local standpoint, this prerequisite was not then carried out. Outside of London the provision as to the Exchanges was practically ignored, with the inevitable result that each locality attacked the

[1] An account of the "Productive Relief Work" policy in post-war Germany is given in Appendix V. It may be contrasted with the summarized program of emergency relief work in Great Britain as given in Appendix VI.

[2] At this time, and for some years afterwards, the term "Labor Exchanges" was generally applied to them.

problem in an isolated, haphazard, and ignorant manner which soon led to disillusionment, in spite of the efforts of a Central Body established to coördinate the work of the Distress Committees. But the returns of such registration offices as were opened for the unemployed, assisted very greatly by collecting information enabling the next experimentation to be more scientific in character.

Thus the first step in separating the problem of unemployment from the general problem of pauperism was taken, and the recognition spread that existing Poor Law methods of dealing with pauperism were actually increasing unemployment among the able-bodied by their "provision of mere subsistence, available when demanded." The Unemployed Workmen Act, by far the most ambitious step yet taken, having been demonstrated as totally inadequate,[1] the period which ensued was one in which past failures and future possibilities were critically analyzed. From this analysis a few major premisses were accepted as sufficiently clear to provide a basis for future policy.

### CONSIDERATIONS WHICH LED TO PRESENT POLICY

It came to be realized, in the first place, that the irregularity of employment which is normal in competitive industry always maintains a majority of workers on the border-line of penury. As a consequence the effect of a period of trade depression is to mingle in one unfortunate mass the so-called "unemployable" and the destitute worker who even in times of general prosperity is only precariously removed from that state. So fine is the distinction between the unemployed and the "employable"[2] that schemes of tiding the former over a depression

[1] J. L. Cohen calls it an "ill-considered, inadequate panic scheme." *Insurance against Unemployment*, p. 165.

[2] War experience has greatly modified the theory that there is a large class of chronic "unemployable." See, for instance, H. A. Mess: *Casual Labor at the Docks*, p. 137.

by short periods of relief work are rendered nugatory. The problem of unemployment, in other words, was recognized to be much more one of regularization in the demand for labor than one of hair-splitting definitions as to the work-capacity of the supply.

A second accepted premiss, more positive in nature, was that unemployment, as a national if not international problem, can never be satisfactorily attacked by purely local efforts. For any remedial treatment which is to be in the least effective there is required a smooth-running and well-integrated national machinery, not only for the purpose of dove-tailing labor supply with labor demand, but even more to afford intelligent information at all times on the changing conditions of employment.

It was further recognized that, however efficient any State machinery of relief might prove, unemployment on a large scale is certain to continue, and to be greatly intensified during depression periods, for at least as long as industry is maintained on its present basis. Therefore, to allay the ill-effects of a certainty which exists for a large percentage of the working class, some form of insurance against unemployment is obviously desirable.

From this there followed the last premiss, that to be effective such insurance must be compulsory, and must be operated through some such nation-wide organization as a uniform Employment Exchange system.

As the existing attempts at solution had ignored every one of these points, it is not surprising that the measures which followed the reports of the Poor Law Commission of 1909, and the publication of various important studies on unemployment, were much more far-reaching than anything which had gone before.

A policy to deal with unemployment must, it was recognized, proceed along two main lines if hope of success was to be entertained therefrom. In the first place, it must endeavor to concentrate and regularize demand; in the second place, it must improve the mobility of supply.

The development of minor palliatives, such as the provision of local relief works, was seen to be futile so long as the two first principles were overlooked. A program of much deeper significance was therefore launched by the State, the success of which may be judged from the sequel. But it may not be premature at this point to observe that, except during the war period, the State has been unable to attack directly the fundamental problem of regularizing the demand for labor. From this impotence arises the conclusion, now steadily gathering force, that solution in this respect is beyond the power of the Collectivist State and must be undertaken by Industry itself.

## THE LABOR EXCHANGES ACT

In September, 1909, the first step in the new policy was taken by the passage of the famous Labor Exchanges Act. This empowered the Board of Trade to establish and maintain Employment Exchanges throughout the country, and to take over the work of the existing Distress Committees. On February 1, 1910, preliminary organization having been accomplished, the twenty exchanges operating in London under the Unemployed Workmen Act were taken over by the Board of Trade, and sixty-three other Exchanges were opened in London and provincial towns. Thus the National Employment Exchange system was launched. By March 31, 1911, 225 Exchanges were in operation and at the outbreak of war, when the scope of the work had been greatly increased by the passage of the first Unemployment Insurance Act, this number had been increased to over 400. The principal objects sought in pressing the Labor Exchanges Act may be summarized as follows: [1]

[1] Cf. Cmd. 1054 (1920), p. 5. But it is to be noted that Lord Askwith, who was in 1909 Comptroller of the Labor and Statistical Departments of the Board of Trade, asserts the Act was modeled largely on German experiments, and was "hastily imposed" upon Great Britain. (Cmd. 1140 (1921), p. 81.) Lord Askwith is an ardent advo-

(1) To provide industry with a State-controlled Employment Service, "free from any form of association with the Poor Law," in order to facilitate equally the placing of unemployed workers and the filling of unoccupied jobs.

(2) To furnish an agency for the operation of a system of compulsory unemployment insurance.

(3) To furnish poorly organized labor with machinery for finding employment, equally effective with that which had been developed independently by the well-organized trade unions.

(4) To provide machinery for improving the mobility of labor, forwarding decasualization experiments, and the more intelligent selection of employment by juveniles.

(5) To collect information as to the course of employment and other labor conditions, enabling the Government to prepare in time for periods of unusual unemployment.

The question whether the National Employment Exchange system was established as a move advisable and sufficient in itself, or in part as a necessary prerequisite to a State scheme of unemployment insurance, is one which has of late aroused some debate. There can be no doubt that the combination was intended by those most instrumental in launching the Employment Exchange system. Sir William Beveridge, who was Director of Labor Exchanges from February, 1910, to the end of 1916, stated categorically to the Committee of Enquiry in 1920 that the second main object for which the Exchanges were instituted was: "to supply the machinery for compulsory unemployment insurance."[1] In its report to Parliament

cate of the theory that the problem of unemployment should be attacked by industries rather than by the State. His assertion that the British system copied that of Germany is vigorously denied by Beveridge (see Cmd. 1140, p. 187).

[1] Cmd. 1140 (1921), p. 180. The first main object as given by Sir William Beveridge was: "to diminish unemployment by reducing the time taken by workmen in looking for work."

this committee observed that "a special feature of the British system of Exchanges" is that "these were founded, not solely or even mainly as placing agencies, but in order to prepare a machinery for the administration of unemployment insurance."[1]

## THE UNION OF EXCHANGES AND INSURANCE

The argument that the Employment Exchanges were established to serve merely as Exchanges, and that the management of unemployment insurance was later grafted on them more or less by hazard, appears to have its origin not in fact, but in a dawning *ex post facto* conclusion that the combination has not been a happy one. While State-operated Unemployment Insurance may need a system of State-operated Employment Exchanges to make it possible, the need is not reciprocal. The essential functions of an Employment Exchange system are entirely clear-cut and straightforward. It is a device designed to achieve a fundamental need — organization of the "labor market," and until that end has been achieved with some adequacy, it is premature to confuse its purpose and operation.

Yet just this confusion has been created by superimposing a cumbersome mass of unemployment insurance machinery on an Employment Exchange system which has never had time and opportunity to achieve its own distinct end. There need be no disposition to criticize the potential efficiency of unemployment insurance as a device for diminishing unemployment to appreciate the havoc which this theory has played in England with the due and necessary development of the Employment Exchanges. In internal organization: in volume of employment work accomplished; in winning the approval of either employers or work-people, the Employment Exchange system in 1923 exhibited an astonishingly small advance over the position reached at the time of the

[1] Cmd. 1054 (1920), p. 10.

passage of the first Unemployment Insurance Act in 1911. It may be confidently asserted that the strain of having to operate the cumbersome and kaleidoscopic series of Unemployment Insurance Acts is largely responsible for this stagnation.

In addition, closer examination will show that the manner in which it has choked the Employment Exchanges is not the only indictment the device of State-operated unemployment insurance must face. Advocates of the scheme have extolled it on the ground that by steadying consumption it actually tends to diminish unemployment.[1] But it is at least assertable that much the same effect might be much more simply attained by the distribution of largesse through the Poor Law Guardians in times of industrial depression. Those who support unemployment insurance as at present operated reply that, as the workers as a class have contributed a large part of the fund from which benefits are drawn, those benefits are (a) preferable to charity on moral grounds, and are (b) a clever device to average earnings for those who are unable or unwilling to provide for the "rainy day." A survey of the operation of unemployment insurance during the post-war depression will show, however, that the payment of benefit has, in the first place, degenerated into what is practically a dole, and has, in the second place, not been able to prevent recourse to additional Poor Law relief by the unemployed in unprecedented numbers. It is because the Employment Exchanges are not functioning properly that the unemployment insurance benefits cannot be increased to an extent which would absorb the amount now being paid by the ratepayer in respect of the additional relief provided by the Poor Law Guardians. At the same time it is largely because of unemployment insurance that the Exchanges are not functioning properly in their true capacity. The vicious

[1] For an effective presentation of this theory see Professor Pigou's *Unemployment*, chap. 13.

circle illustrates the futility of the present combination of ineffective Exchanges and ineffective insurance.

Unfortunate as is the present situation a "remedy" not infrequently proposed is more unfortunate still. Natural unrest caused by accumulating evidence that the Exchanges are not what they should be sometimes forms itself into an unreasoning attack on the very existence of the Exchanges. Abolition of the machinery, and not of the causes which render that machinery ineffectual, is demanded. Indeed, the one factor that has insured continuation of the Exchanges during the post-war economy campaign is, strange to say, realization that the Unemployment Insurance Acts could not operate without them. The very development which has prevented the Exchanges from being what they should is, by strange irony, the reason most strongly advocated against their dissolution. The oak is spared in order not to interfere with the ivy which is killing it.

# CHAPTER II

## THE ADVENT OF STATE-OPERATED UNEMPLOY-
## MENT INSURANCE

In closing their chapter on "Insurance," in *The Prevention of Destitution*, Mr. and Mrs. Sidney Webb, at the time of the passage of the first National Insurance Act, made the following prediction as to the future of State-operated compulsory unemployment insurance:

> Whatever scheme of insurance is adopted — especially a bad scheme — will plainly not be final. We shall have to learn from our own experience, if we are too foolish to learn by the experience of others; and we shall find, as the German Government has found, that insurance schemes are always in the melting pot.[1]

In retrospect from the situation in Great Britain thirteen years after these words were written, this statement, with the closely reasoned argument which leads up to it, is a notable example of verified prophecy. In the decade from July, 1912, to July, 1922, seven major Acts on unemployment insurance, not to mention a number of minor ones, were brought into operation. Five of these were passed after August, 1920, under the unprecedented pressure of the period of post-war depression, and resulted in so defacing the principles of the program that "insurance" became a word applicable only by courtesy. Elasticity in any scheme of unemployment insurance is, of course, essential. The scale of contributions and benefits should both be subject to revision in order to maintain the insurance fund in solvency. It is obvious that no scheme of unemployment insurance could have passed through the post-war period unaltered and unscathed.

[1] The reference is to State insurance against sickness, accident, invalidity, and old age, in Germany. There is no State-operated system of unemployment insurance in Germany.

But it is equally obvious that a program which goes to pieces as this one did is far from the valuable device it seemed before its time of testing came.

### THE FIRST UNEMPLOYMENT INSURANCE ACT

The first Unemployment Insurance Act (technically it was Part II of the National Insurance Act of 1911, Part I dealing with insurance against sickness) was passed by Parliament in December, 1911, and came into operation on July 15, 1912, the National Employment Exchange system being then two and one half years old. The trades selected for the experiment were ones in which unemployment is normally not only high, but also subject to seasonal and cyclical fluctuations. They were seven in number: Building, Construction of Works, Shipbuilding, Mechanical Engineering, Ironfounding, Vehicle Construction, and Sawmilling, the persons affected therein being all manual workers and other workers in receipt of less than £160 per annum. About 2,250,000 workpeople of sixteen and upwards were thus compulsorily included at the outset, of whom all but a very small fraction were males. Less than one fifth of this number had been previously insured against unemployment through voluntary associations.

Of the three parties to financial contribution, the State took smallest part, its share being 1.67*d.* per week in respect of each insured workman. Each workman contributed 2.5*d.* per week; the employer the same sum for every insured employee. Thus the proportion of the State contribution to that of industry was one third (reduced to one quarter in 1920). No benefits were payable until the scheme had been in operation for six months, when insured persons were eligible for benefit at the rate of seven shillings per week,[1] provided they had been

[1] Half this sum for insured persons under eighteen years of age. The weekly rate of contribution in respect of these was: State, .67*d.*; employer, 1*d.*; employed person, 1*d.*

unemployed for a week, had registered and deposited the individual unemployment book at an Employment Exchange, had shown they were not out of work voluntarily without just cause, or on account of misconduct or a trade dispute, and were not in receipt of illness benefit under Part I of the Act. Payment of benefit then depended on the unemployed worker being ready at any time to accept a job offered through the Labor Exchange, provided:

(a) That the offer of employment was not for a situation vacant in consequence of a trade dispute.

(b) That an offer of employment in the district where he was last ordinarily employed, or in any other district, was not for a rate of wage lower or conditions less favorable than the prevailing standard for the employment in question.

It was further laid down that the decision on a claim to benefit should be made in the first instance by an insurance officer appointed by the Board of Trade, one or more members of the staff of each Employment Exchange having delegated authority in this capacity. Any workman considering that his claim to benefit has been refused, or stopped, for insufficient reasons, may appeal to a Court of Referees consisting of an equal number of representatives of employers and workmen presided over by a chairman appointed by the Board of Trade.[1] If the insurance officer disagrees with the recommendation of this court, he must, if required by the court, refer the matter to the umpire, a Crown official whose decision in contested claims is final, as was his decision on questions of whether or not a workman came within the scope of the Act until a new determination on questions of insurability was laid down by the Act of 1920. (See p. 36.)

[1] The present tense is used in cases where the original rulings have not been modified, in any important respect, by subsequent legislation. At the beginning of 1917 the newly established Ministry of Labor took over all duties with respect to unemployment previously handled by the Board of Trade.

In addition to the disqualifications for benefit summarized above, two very important limitations were laid down, designed to confine benefits to those unemployed through trade fluctuations and prevent a drain on the fund by those unemployed through personal deficiencies. These limitations were:

(1) Benefits could not be obtained for more than fifteen weeks in any period of twelve months.

(2) Five weeks' contributions were established as a prerequisite for one week's benefit.

The Unemployment Fund was to be managed and controlled by the Board of Trade. Advances to the fund up to £3,000,000 could be obtained from the Treasury provided that, so long as any such advance was outstanding, the Treasury could restore the fund to solvency by modifying the rates of contribution, or the rates or periods of benefit, within specified limits. Up to ten per cent of the receipts from the industrial contributions — that is, .5d. per insured person per week — could be applied by order of the Treasury towards administrative expenses.

The method established for collecting contributions is similar to that used for the Health Insurance Scheme, and has operated with only minor changes from the outset. On application at the Employment Exchange, Unemployment Books are issued direct to all insured workers. During employment these books are kept by the employer; during unemployment, they are lodged at the Exchange. Before each payment of wages the employer affixes to these books the appropriate value of Unemployment Insurance stamps, on sale at all post-offices, recovering the employed person's share of contribution by deduction from the pay envelope. While these deductions cannot be made retroactive, employers are permitted to make arrangements whereby books are stamped quarterly or half-yearly with high-value stamps.

The above measures provided the bare machinery for launching compulsory unemployment insurance in the seven selected trades. The Act of 1911, however, contained further important provisions. Entirely apart from the insurance function, several measures specifically designed to reduce unemployment were included. To discourage casual employment the rate of employers' and workers' contributions for periods of employment of less than a week in duration was raised above the average daily rate taking the week as a unit. To encourage the employer in giving permanent employment, a refund was allowed in respect of every workman continuously employed for a year, equal to one third of the contributions paid by the employer on his own behalf in respect of such workman. In practice this condition led to serious difficulties, owing to such interruptions to continuous employment as fires or strikes. Another refund was allowed to employers who instituted systematic short-time during periods of depression. An employee who at the age of sixty had made five hundred or more weekly payments could personally (or in case of death his representatives) reclaim from the fund that part of the sum contributed over and above amounts already returned in benefit, plus compound interest at two and one half per cent.[1]

A third group of measures was aimed to encourage voluntary unemployment insurance among associations of work-people. Two separate steps, the first concerned with work-people already insured, the second for any association of work-people, were taken towards this end:

(1) Insured trade unions were allowed to pay the State benefit of seven shillings a week direct to their members (the joint contributions of employers and workmen still being payable to the State) and periodically to recover from the Unemployment Fund the amount so paid. A trade union could thus pay as large a compound benefit as it desired, recovering up to seven shillings per week

[1] For an estimate of the success of these complicated provisions see p. 38.

per member receiving benefit. On the other hand, in no case might the State repayment exceed three fourths of the total payments made by the union to its unemployed members. It will be seen that such arrangement depended on the association paying at least two shillings four pence a week unemployment benefit to qualified members out of its own funds. (Seven shillings = three fourths of nine shillings four pence.)

(2) The "Ghent system" of direct subvention to trade-union funds was for the first time introduced into Great Britain. The Act provided that the State would repay up to one sixth of the total benefit paid by "any association of persons not trading for profit" to its unemployed members, in respect of benefits not exceeding twelve shillings a week. Trade unions covering about 1,500,000 members received subventions, amounting in all to £282,-307, under this scheme, while insured workers, whose numbers varied from 540,000 in 1913 to 1,448,000 in 1919, received the State benefit through their own unions. A number of State-insured workers were able, indirectly, to take advantage of both measures.

The Act gave the Board of Trade authority, with the consent of the Treasury, to make an order extending its scope to other trades. Finally, there should be mentioned a provision designed to encourage utilization of the Employment Exchanges by employers, whereby the Exchange not only undertook for each employer coöperating much of the clerical work involved in the Act, but also arranged to treat all the periods of employment of the same or different workmen engaged through the Exchange as a continuous employment of one workman so far as the employers' contributions were concerned.

## FEATURES OF THE ACT OF 1911

The features of this very complex measure will be seen to fall naturally into five heads: Compulsion; Subvention; Contribution; Prevention; and Limitation. Some further analysis of each of these is necessary to bring out more plainly the scope and intention of this parent Act.

COMPULSION. By pooling good risks and bad risks, the Act sought to even to some extent the menace of unemployment for all members of insured trades. This was a cardinal feature maintained throughout all subsequent legislation. It is worth remarking at this point that, considered in its simplest aspect, unemployment insurance is no more a preventive of the contingency insured against than insurances against fire, sickness, or shipwreck are preventives of those risks. To some extent insurance actually encourages a more frequent occurrence of the contingency insured against. Herein lay a main reason for coupling unemployment insurance with a national system of Employment Exchanges. Through the Exchanges checks against fraud could be put in operation.

SUBVENTION. In order not to affect adversely individual characteristics of thrift and foresight, the Act, while accepting the principle of compulsion, sought also to encourage voluntary unemployment insurance both among those insured by the State and among those to whom the Government measure did not extend.

CONTRIBUTION. Workman, employer, and State were all involved in the contributory scheme; the measure of respective contribution being chosen arbitrarily and admittedly experimentally. The principal arguments for the inclusion of all three parties may be summarized as follows: *Workman* — (a) to encourage a personal interest in the success of the experiment; (b) to prevent the payment of benefit having any charitable aspect; (c) to attempt an averaging of earnings between good times and bad times. *Employer* — (a) as a recognition of the partial responsibility of the individual employer for much avertible unemployment; (b) to give him a direct financial interest in reducing this type of unemployment to a minimum. *State* — (a) to justify the necessary elements of control;

(b) to acknowledge the partial responsibility of the community as a whole for unemployment.

PREVENTION. The elaborate system of refunds was included with the specific intention of reducing unemployment. The refund to employers for workmen continuously employed, as also the extra contributions for employment of less than a week's duration, were designed to discourage casual employment. The refund for the institution of systematic short-time was designed to encourage an elasticity in working hours which would diffuse rather than concentrate inevitable unemployment. The refund to workmen with good employment records was meant to encourage extra effort on the part of the employee to maintain himself in regular work.

LIMITATION. While compelling all those in insured trades to contribute to the Unemployment Fund, the Act was carefully safeguarded with the hope of limiting the payment of benefit to those unemployed solely because of economic conditions over which they had no control. In addition to disqualifications directed against those unemployed because of desire, ill-health, misconduct, or even because of a trade dispute, there were added the limitations already stated: (1) proof of fairly regular prior employment in an insured trade; (2) a maximum period for which benefit could be paid; (3) five weeks of contribution as a prerequisite for one of benefit. The design of all these safeguards was to prevent malingering and to provide an automatic check against the "unemployable" receiving support from the Insurance Fund.

### THE SUCCESSFUL LAUNCHING OF INSURANCE

Such, so far as all essentials, was the Unemployment Insurance Act of 1911. It is unnecessary, for present purposes, to examine in detail the early operation of the scheme. Heroic and successful efforts were made by a necessarily inexperienced staff to launch an organization for which there was no precedent in history, and as a result compulsory State insurance against unemployment was definitely proved to be administratively practical. From the beginning income exceeded outlay, that pleasant condition continuing until the post-war depression. The early effect of the compulsory scheme was actually to encourage additional voluntary insurance. So well thought-out and planned was this initial legislation that for a long time no amendments except on a few points of administrative detail were deemed advisable. Difficulties regarding the definition and the test of unemployment, as well as scores of minor obstacles, were found in practice to be surmountable. So long as conditions of trade continued good, the Act prospered, and such saturnine forebodings as that cited at the beginning of this chapter appeared on the surface to have been completely refuted. Even when the post-war period of depression was well started, one enthusiastic advocate of compulsory State insurance felt justified in writing that "the main difficulties have been overcome." [1]

And yet, signs were not lacking that judgments based on this halcyon period of initial success would prove pitifully premature. One ominous indication was the way in which the immature Employment Exchanges were, by the pressure of insurance work, hampered from developing the technique and efficiency necessary for their fundamental duty of filling the greatest possible number of vacancies with suitable workers. There was also the obvious fact that, given a protracted period of depression, the seven shillings a week of benefit would by itself be inadequate even to prevent starvation. Yet knowledge that the Employment Exchange system was not sufficiently developed to bring the contingency insured against to as quick an end as possible forced the benefit for all to be kept well below the returns to the very worst-paid labor. A third sign of latent trouble was the fact that even

---

[1] J. L. Cohen, in the preface to his *Insurance against Unemployment*.

with this low and much restricted benefit an average
unemployment of seven and one half per cent — by no
means unprecedented even in pre-war days[1] — would have
sufficed to make expenditure exceed income, making no
allowance for administrative expense.

Fortunate, and yet unfortunate, for the scheme of
compulsory insurance was it that the introduction coincided with a period of unusually good employment, and
that this period carried over almost without a break
into the war, when for more than four years unemployment nearly ceased to exist. "The good state of trade
during the past year," wrote the Director of Labor Exchanges in July, 1913, "has contributed perhaps more
than any other single fact to making it administratively
possible to launch the scheme of unemployment insurance
at all." [2] Those in control of the system at that time were
men with the capacity to look and plan ahead. As the
1913 report on the workings of the first Unemployment
Insurance Act shows, they did not rely too heavily on
temporary assets. It is just possible that with the same
guiding minds that brought it into being, State-operated
unemployment insurance in Great Britain might have
been so directed as to have weathered the unprecedented
depression of the post-war period.

To the depressing record of degeneration which, when
the storm broke, overwhelmed this social experiment
of so much interest and promise, it will, after tracing the
intermediate steps of importance, be necessary to turn.

[1] Reference to the chart following p. 71 will show that the trade-
union percentage of unemployment reached or exceeded 7.5 in eight
of the thirty-seven years from 1875 to 1912.

[2] Cmd. 6965 (1913), p. 46.

# CHAPTER III

## UNEMPLOYMENT INSURANCE DURING THE WAR AND DEMOBILIZATION

JULY, 1912, to July, 1914, the first two years of State Unemployment Insurance in Great Britain, were also years in which unemployment was at a minimum in that country. The mean unemployed percentage during the decade 1903–1913 among trade unions making returns to the Board of Trade had been 4.9. During the twenty-four months ending July, 1914, the corresponding percentage never rose above 2.6 and kept a mean of 2.1. Consequently it is not surprising that the first amending Act, which was before Parliament when war broke out, should only have applied modifications which, compared with the changes to come later, were of negligible importance. The times were exceptionally good, the initial Act was working as well as its most optimistic supporters had dared to hope, and points of administrative detail were in the main the only ones on which amendment seemed advisable.

The few noteworthy revisions in the original Act brought about by the National Insurance (Part II, Amendment) Act of 1914 are quickly summarized. Section 1 amended the statutory conditions for the receipt of unemployment benefit by substituting a minimum of ten contributions as a condition of eligibility instead of the previous rule of twenty-six separate weeks of employment in the preceding five years. Sections 5 and 6 made certain alterations in the system of refunds, of which the most important was the substitution of a flat refund to the employer of three shillings per annum for the clause which had provided for the refund of one third of contributions paid in respect of a workman continuously employed.

A simple calculation shows that this revision slightly reduced the amount of refund payable to the employer on the ground of continuous employment. [1] To meet the difficulty of interruptions to continuous employment beyond control of the employer, the term was redefined as meaning forty-five or more weekly contributions per annum. Section 7 granted exemption from contribution (instead of refund) for workmen and employer in the case of approved systematic short-time schemes during "exceptional unemployment." Finally, section 14 considerably increased the amount of "Ghent system" subventions by removing the limitation to the sum on which the State would repay one sixth of benefit, merely providing that at rates of benefit exceeding seventeen shillings a week the amount of State subvention should "be subject to such reduction [if any] as the Board [of Trade] may think just."

### Demarcation under Partial Insurance

With the single exception that eligibility to benefit was made somewhat less rigorous, the 1914 Act entailed no alterations of moment in the original plan. More important than the alterations which were made was the pleasant discovery that certain problems which had seemed almost insurmountable in theory were by no means insoluble in practice. Chief of these was the, at first sight, seemingly impossible task of demarcation — of separating out the workmen who from one point of view were members of one of the seven insured trades, but who from another point of view were engaged in an uninsured occupation. As the demarcation difficulty is one which is advanced as a convincing argument against the feasibility of insurance by industry, it is important to recognize

[1] Under the original Act the employer's contribution in respect of a workman continuously employed for one year was $2.5d. \times 52$, or $130d$. The refund of one third, therefore, equaled $43\frac{1}{3}d.$, or $7\frac{1}{3}d.$ more than the three shillings substituted by the Act of 1914.

with what success the same problem was met when State insurance against unemployment was confined to a few trades.

Under the Act of 1911, as already stated, it was provided that demarcation questions should be dealt with by an umpire appointed by the Crown and independent of the authority responsible for the administration of unemployment insurance. Provision whereby any workman or employer could bring a contentious case, with right of giving evidence, directly before the umpire, was made in regulations adopted by the Board of Trade in March, 1912, and the first decision was handed down at the end of the following month. In the next fifteen months over twelve hundred decisions raising questions of general interest and establishing precedents were published, the majority of them being demarcation questions. Once a body of precedent had been brought together, the number of demarcation cases referred to the umpire rapidly diminished.

The Board of Trade Report on the operation of the Unemployment Insurance Act of 1911 up to July, 1913, pointed out that special difficulties of demarcation arose among certain classes of workmen, specifically as to distinctions on the margin of the furnishing (uninsured) and building (insured) trades. Nevertheless, even at the end of a single year of operation, the conclusion of the Director of Labor Exchanges was that "some sort of demarcation of the insured trades has been effected." [1] While it would be idle to deny that difficulties of demarcation continued as long as some trades were insured and others not, the difficulties were never of an insoluble nature. Moreover, they diminished with gratifying rapidity as a body of precedent, laid down by an impartial arbiter, was collected. Even by the time of the 1914 Act the problem of demarcation had ceased to be a very formidable one.

[1] Cmd. 6965 (1913), p. 46. Cf. also p. 11 of that document.

FAILURE TO EXTEND INSURANCE DURING THE WAR

The war period was, of course, one in which unemployment temporarily ceased to be a problem. Even by contrast with the two unusually good years which had preceded, the state of employment was unprecedented.[1] At the beginning of 1915 the trade-union percentage of unemployment had fallen below 2.0 and it continued below that figure, even falling for months at a stretch below .5 per cent, until the end of 1918. Manifestly such an opportunity was invaluable for building up the Insurance Fund and otherwise preparing for the inevitable period of reckoning after the war. Much bitter criticism has been directed at the neglect of the Government to seize this opportunity, and although an important preparatory step was taken by the National Insurance (Part II, Munition Workers) Act of 1916, the complete failure to follow this up until too late proved fatal.

Nevertheless, criticisms directed against the Government for letting slip this golden opportunity to improve the position of national unemployment insurance, are misplaced. What the Webbs call the hypertrophied political institutions of to-day are not the form of social machinery from which far-sighted planning is to be expected at the best of times.[2] During the war all the energies of an overburdened Government were necessarily concentrated on other subjects than the extension of insurance against unemployment, particularly as unemployment at the time was almost non-existent. Criticism that the Government did not at this period prepare for the coming crisis is shallow. The real charge, too often overlooked, is that a modern bureaucracy, working through parliamentary government, is always so much involved

[1] See Table V, p. 71.
[2] There is much that is apposite to any consideration of the most effective form of unemployment relief in the Webbs' *A Constitution for the Socialist Commonwealth of Great Britain*. See especially chap. 3 therein.

in the multitudinous problems of the present as to be virtually incapable of preparing for the future hazards of industrial life.

## THE ACT OF 1916

The second important Unemployment Insurance Act, that of 1916, extended the provisions of the original Act to all workers engaged on, or in connection with, munitions work who were not already insured. The term "munitions" was made widely inclusive and the trades added to the insured list were: Metal Trades; Ammunition and Explosives; Chemicals; Leather and Leather Goods; Rubber and Rubber Manufactures; Brick, Tile, and Stone; Army Clothing and similar manufactures. The number of insured work-people was thus increased by about one and a half million, making a total of nearly four million, of whom approximately one quarter were now women. [1] Substantially, these trades were simply added to those insured under the parent Act of 1911, the amounts of financial contribution and benefit, and the principles of operation being unaltered. The Act was designed as a temporary measure, limited in its duration to not more than three years after the close of the war. It remained on the statute books until superseded by the Act of 1920.

Underlying the 1916 Act was the anticipation that transition from war to peace would see a period of severe unemployment in the munition trades. By insuring the munition workers while they were in full employment contributions would mount up to a sum enabling the Insurance Fund to withstand the post-war strain. On the same reasoning it was urged prior to the 1916 Act, and continually afterwards, that it was illogical to stop

[1] The estimates of the number insured by the Act of 1916 differ somewhat, as is natural considering the war-time expansion in the industries listed above. The Ministry of Labor states that the number of work-people insured under this Act rose from 1,089,000 at January, 1917, to 1,417,000 at July, 1918.

short after insuring four million workers, or less than one third of the industrial population. In February, 1918, one of the Ministry of Reconstruction's advisory committees[1] reported that "unless a scheme of general insurance is devised and launched at the earliest possible date, it may be impossible to avoid the disastrous chaos of unorganized and improvised methods of relieving distress," a warning which was endorsed by most of those who knew anything about the unemployment insurance program. There can be no doubt that had a higher rate of contribution been levied in this time of fictitious prosperity, and had all trades been compulsorily insured, the fund would have been so augmented as to have delayed materially the *débâcle* into which the post-war depression plunged the State program.[2]

As it was, not only was nothing else of importance done for unemployment insurance during the war period, with the result that the Armistice system of outright donations had to be hurriedly set up, but even the whole of the two years of active trade which succeeded the war was allowed to pass before the over-delayed Act of 1920 was brought into being.

Before coming to the demobilization period, however, it is advisable to complete the record of unemployment insurance legislation prior to the Act of 1920.

[1] The Unemployment Insurance Sub-Committee of the Civil War Workers' Committee. In 1917 the Labor Party published a lengthy statement on "The Prevention of Unemployment After the War." "It is necessary," this said, "that the Government should have settled, in advance, a systematic plan for dealing with the unemployment that is threatened — rather than wait until it occurs and then meet it by charitable doles and other emergency measures." In 1923 the Ministry of Labor asserted that "the extension of 1916 to trades largely engaged in making munitions was probably the widest which industrial opinion would then have supported." (*Report on National Unemployment Insurance to July, 1923*, p. 6.)

[2] This argument is taken up at some length in Chapter VI, pp. 74 to 77.

## OTHER ACTS PRIOR TO 1920

The New Ministries and Secretaries Act of 1916, while having no direct bearing on the State program of unemployment relief, established the Ministry of Labor as a separate department and transferred to it from the Board of Trade all powers and duties of Government relating to labor and industry. The actual transference took place on January 10, 1917, from which date management of the Employment Exchanges and State-operated Unemployment Insurance has been under the Ministry of Labor.

The National Insurance (Unemployment) Act of 1918 was a brief and superfluous measure which gave the Minister of Labor power to cancel any of the extensions made in the 1916 Act if, "having regard to the prospects of unemployment . . . at the end of the war," he saw fit. Just as brief was the National Insurance (Unemployment) Act, 1919, passed on December 23d of that year, which increased the rate of benefit to eleven shillings a week (half this sum for insured persons under eighteen), an amount which, because of the depreciation in the value of money during the war, represented less purchasing power than the original benefit allowance of seven shillings a week. This nominal increase in benefit, however, was not accompanied by any increase in the amount of contributions to the Insurance Fund, and thereby helped to hasten the state of insolvency into which the Fund was now soon to be plunged.

Nevertheless, as the following table will show, the Insurance Fund at this time appeared superficially in very healthy condition, the protracted period of good employment having by July 12, 1919, piled up a balance of £18,000,000 in spite of the Government's refusal to take any steps other than those provided by the Act of 1916 to accumulate a heavy reserve in anticipation of bad times to come. In January, 1921, the Fund attained its maximum amount — £22,750,000. The rapidity with which this large surplus was transformed into a deficit by the depression indicates the underlying insecurity of the national unemployment insurance program. It proved a child of fair weather, incapable of withstanding a period of storm. The accumulated reserves of eight years of abnormally good employment vanished like smoke under the stress of six abnormally bad months.

TABLE I.    THE UNEMPLOYMENT FUND FROM 1913 TO 1923

| Insurance Year Ending Mid-July | Contributions from | | Benefits Paid Out | Balance of Unemployment Fund | Contribution from Fund towards Cost of Administration e | Total Cost of Administration f |
| | Employers and Work-People | State | | | | |
|---|---|---|---|---|---|---|
| 1913 | £1,622,038 | £378,000a | £208,318 | Surplus £1,648,907 | £151,200a | £379,859a |
| 1914 | 1,802,940 | 602,000 | 530,593 | " 3,211,401 | 246,410 | 558,053 |
| 1915 | 1,649,641 | 546,666 | 418,701 | " 4,724,124 | 227,281 | 553,606 |
| 1916 | 1,694,115 | 538,863 | 78,985 | " 6,711,504 | 231,298 | 450,941 |
| 1917 | 2,699,932 | 746,372 | 34,312 | " 10,075,467 | 329,466 | 481,795 |
| 1918 | 3,277,123 | 1,007,541 | 86,159 | " 14,222,112 | 444,784 | 597,863 |
| 1919 | 2,871,640 | 994,402 | 152,721 | " 18,030,356 | 455,401 | 698,713 |
| 1920 | 3,043,252 | 912,701 | 1,009,126 | " 21,287,648 | 448,744 | 558,262 |
| 1921 | 11,303,175b | 2,168,639 | 34,118,195 | " 99,798 | 1,098,592 | 2,541,700 |
| 1922 | 31,166,275b | 11,057,901c | 52,848,214 | Deficit 15,386,188 | 4,838,136d | 7,299,322 |
| 1923 | 34,053,304b | 12,465,682 | 41,878,667 | " 16,342,526 | 4,782,500 | 4,782,500 |

a The State contributions and the sums listed in the last two columns are for the fiscal year April 1 to March 31, with the two exceptions listed in footnotes c and d. All other figures are for the insurance year which ended in mid-July, until 1921, since then ending the beginning of July.

b Employers' and work-peoples' contributions under 1921, 1922, and 1923 include £2,666,805 paid to the Fund by the Naval and Military establishments (under Section 41 of the 1920 Act) for the purpose of qualifying ex-service men to receive unemployment benefit.

c The State grant for the period April–July, 1922, was received during the insurance year 1921–22.

d The Contribution towards Cost of Administration for the period April–July, 1922, was paid during the insurance year 1921–22.

e By the Act of 1920 one tenth, and by the Act of April, 1922, one eighth, of the income of the Unemployment Fund, has been applicable to administrative expenses. In the fiscal year ending March 31, 1923, administrative expenses were 10.3 per cent of income. This was the first year in which they were completely covered by the revenue of the Fund.

f Including cost of the Employment Exchanges as placing agencies so far as they deal with insured persons.

## OUT-OF-WORK DONATIONS

Demobilization brought the first definite evidence that the Government system of unemployment insurance was incapable of standing any unusual strain. Partly because not more than one third of industrial workers were at that time covered by State unemployment insurance, partly because the maximum benefit of eleven shillings a week was quite inadequate in view of living costs, a scheme of free out-of-work donation was hastily established for substantially all of those who were thrown out of employment by the cessation of hostilities. Monetary grants for soldiers unemployed in the period immediately following discharge had been foreshadowed by the Government in December, 1915, but the decision to make these grants applicable to civilians was unexpected in view of the purpose of the Act of 1916. The scheme was one of doles, pure and simple; the financing was separately budgeted and did not come out of the Insurance Fund; and the effect, since insured work-people could draw this higher donation without exhausting their rights to the regular insurance benefit (though both could not be drawn at the same time), was to relegate the whole system of insurance to a position of secondary importance. A very little experience with Out-of-Work Donation (O.W.D., as it came to be known) foreshadowed a new economic theory somewhat akin to Gresham's Law — that doles drive out unemployment insurance.

The original O.W.D. scheme, coming into effect on November 25, 1918, and designed to last only twelve months in the case of ex-service men and six months in the case of civilians, provided allowances at the rate of twenty-nine shillings per week for men, twenty-five shillings a week for women, and half those amounts respectively for boys and girls, together with additional allowances for dependent children under fifteen.[1] Payment of the donation was limited to thirteen weeks in the case of civilians and to twenty-six weeks in the case of ex-service men, although in the case of the latter it might be extended for another thirteen weeks (twenty weeks in the case of disabled men) at a slightly reduced rate. Commissioned officers were not eligible. Recipients of

[1] Six shillings a week for the first child, and three shillings a week for each additional child.

O.W.D. were required to sign on regularly at the Employment Exchanges, and accept any suitable employment offered them.

The belief that this scheme of doles, once under way, could be abruptly terminated at the end of six months or a year was optimistic. As a matter of fact, it was extended no less than four times, with alterations the chief effect of which was to exclude all but ex-service men and merchant seamen, and to somewhat decrease the amount while lengthening the period of donation. Thus Out-of-Work Donation, Special Extension Scheme No. 3, which operated from August 2, 1920, to November 6, 1920, provided for unemployed ex-service men and merchant seamen donations of twenty shillings per week for men and fifteen shillings per week for women over a period of fourteen weeks. As the period of the third extension was two days short of fourteen calendar weeks, continuous donation was given, and it is of interest to note that this principle was accepted in the case of ex-service men even before the post-war depression had really arrived. The number receiving this continuous benefit, however, did not rise to much above 200,000, many of whom were partially disabled.

Officially, Out-of-Work Donation came to a close at the end of the fourth Special Extension Scheme on March 31, 1921, although those whose original O.W.D. policies had not then expired continued in diminishing numbers to draw payment for some months. It was not until December 28, 1922, more than four years after the Armistice, that the last individual payment of donation was made. From March 4, 1921, to February 7, 1922, the numbers drawing O.W.D. decreased from 355,783 to 18, and in budgeting for the fiscal year ending March 31, 1923, the Minister of Labor was able to estimate O.W.D. costs at only £7500 as against £438,175 for the fiscal year 1921–22.[1] The total amount of Out-of-Work Donation

[1] Estimates for Civil Services for the Year Ending March 31, 1923, Class VII, p. 39.

paid was approximately £61,659,000, of which civilians received £21,725,000. In addition the cost of O.W.D. administration amounted to about £4,400,000.[1] It was fortunate for the Insurance Fund that it was not drawn upon for any of this expenditure of £66,000,000.

The inadequacy of existing State-operated unemployment insurance at a time of very great social strain and unrest had necessitated the thoroughly unsatisfactory and extravagant scheme of O.W.D. Appreciation of the uneconomic nature of doles, strengthened by evidences (on the whole surprisingly few) of fraudulent abuse of O.W.D., now enlisted recruits for a hopelessly belated but determined effort to bolster up insurance as a bulwark of defense against unemployment. The extent to which this had been forgotten during the period of demobilization may be seen by the figures of those receiving O.W.D. during 1919, a year in which industry was experiencing considerable, if short-lived, prosperity, and in which the mean trade-union percentage of unemployment was only 2.4.

TABLE II.   NUMBERS RECEIVING OUT-OF-WORK DONATION DURING 1919

| DATE | CIVILIANS | EX-SERVICE | TOTAL |
|---|---|---|---|
| 1919 | | | |
| January 3 . . . . | 334,820 | 22,333 | 357,153 |
| February 7 . . . . | 608,629 | 58,655 | 667,284 |
| March 7 . . . . . | 722,205 | 177,990 | 900,195 |
| April 4 . . . . . | 718,154 | 304,988 | 1,023,142 |
| May 2 . . . . . . | 664,762 | 361,733 | 1,026,495 |
| June 6 . . . . . . | 306,616 | 341,298 | 647,194 |
| July 4 . . . . . . | 196,945 | 322,097 | 519,042 |
| August 1 . . . . . | 174,441 | 322,580 | 497,021 |
| September 5 . . . | 111,314 | 286,245 | 397,559 |
| October 10 . . . . | 95,748 | 299,781 | 395,529 |
| November 7 . . . | 132,766 | 305,226 | 437,992 |
| December 5 . . . | . . . . | 319,378 | 319,378 |
| 1920 | | | |
| January 2 . . . . | . . . . | 353,057 | 353,057 |

In February, 1919, confronted by the fact that more

[1] *Labor Gazette*, November, 1923, p. 394.

than ten times as many civilians as ex-service men were receiving donations, a "National Conference of Employers and Employed," called by the Prime Minister, resolved "that the normal provision for maintenance during unemployment should be more adequate and of wider application than is provided by the existing National Insurance Acts." A bill for a much more universal system of unemployment insurance was then promised by the Government and, after nine months had been utilized in the drafting and other delays, the measure was introduced in the House of Commons in November, 1919. Here it was held over until the following session and was presented again, in somewhat altered form, in February, 1920. Following a further delay[1] of half a year, the bill was enacted into law on August 9, 1920, just as it was beginning to be realized that a depression of unusual severity was about to settle on the country. When the Act of 1920 came into operation, on November 8th of that year, the depression had already set in.

[1] These delays are an example of what is meant by the "hypertrophy of political institutions." In November, 1918, the official *Labor Gazette* had stated (p. 437) that it was the intention "to press forward" universal contributory insurance "and to introduce it as early as possible."

# CHAPTER IV

## THE ACT OF 1920 AND THE BEGINNINGS OF INSURANCE BY INDUSTRY

THE Unemployment Insurance Act of 1920 was by far the most imposing legislation of its kind since the parent Act of 1911, and was in several important respects designed as an entirely new charter for unemployment insurance. Its provisions occupied forty-eight printed pages, many of them drawn with a view to permanency which appears pathetic in light of the sequel. For example, Section 16 stated that "if at any time after the expiration of seven years from the commencement of this Act it appears to the Minister that the unemployment fund is insufficient or more than sufficient to discharge the liabilities imposed . . . the Minister may . . . revise the rates of contribution of employers and employed persons under this Act. . . . " The Act had not been in operation four months before contributions and benefits were both revised. By the time the 1920 Act was twenty-eight months old, it had been amended and emasculated by no less than five separate measures of importance. Many of its provisions have thereby been reduced to items of historical interest only. In principles of operation the Act of 1920 was based on that of 1911, and for present purposes it will be sufficient to point out the major revisions made in the parent Act and what they involved.

### CHANGES BROUGHT BY THE ACT OF 1920

The basic design was to extend widely the system of State-operated compulsory unemployment insurance. The full list of employments excepted from the scope of the Act is given in Appendix I, but broadly speaking it may be said that all manual workers were included except those engaged in agriculture,[1] domestic service, the fighting forces, and those engaged by a public authority or public utility company and not subject to dismissal except for misconduct or neglect of duty. Non-manual workers employed for less than £250 per annum, excepting teachers and agents paid by commission or profit-sharing, were also included. About twelve million persons of sixteen years of age and upwards, of whom nearly one third were women, were now compulsorily insured by the State, this number representing approximately two thirds of the total occupied population of the country.[2]

Certificates exempting individual insured persons from paying contributions and receiving benefit are granted under Section 3 of this Act to those who have private means available in case of complete unemployment. Up to July, 1923, exemption certificates to the number of 37,300 had been granted, for the most part on the ground of possession of private income or pension of £26 a year or upward. In all such cases of exemption the employer continues to pay his full share of contribution, the State paying something less than half of its normal contribution. There seems to be real inequity in this ruling that the employer must pay contributions for the small minority

---

[1] A committee representing employers and workers in agriculture, appointed by the Agricultural Wages Board "to inquire into and report upon the extent to which the Unemployment Insurance Act might be made applicable and beneficial to agricultural workers," submitted its report in July, 1921 (Cmd. 1344). The general conclusions of this Committee were (1) that in most districts the large majority of farm workers are in constant employment year after year; (2) that few farmers or agricultural laborers utilize the Employment Exchanges; (3) that there was general opposition, both by employers and workers, to the inclusion of agriculture under the general provisions of the 1920 Act. None of these reasons are very convincing. Certainly none of them would interfere with the introduction of the principle of insurance by industry in agriculture.

[2] The Act of 1920, in other words, added about eight million workpeople to the four million, or thereabouts, already insured against unemployment by the State.

of employees so favorably situated as not to need unemployment insurance.

Weekly contributions and maximum weekly benefit under the 1920 Act were as follows:

|  | MEN | WOMEN | BOYS | GIRLS |
|---|---|---|---|---|
|  |  |  | (16 and 17 years of age) | |
| State contribution . . . . | 2d. | 1.67d. | 1.33d. | 1d. |
| Employed person . . . . | 4d. | 3d. | 2d. | 1.5d. |
| Employer . . . . . . . . | 4d. | 3.5d. | 2d. | 2d. |
| Total contribution in respect of an individual | 10d. | 8.17d. | 5.33d. | 4.5d. |
| Maximum weekly benefit . | 15s. | 12s. | 7s. 6d. | 6s. |

In general, the regulations for registration at an Employment Exchange on becoming unemployed and acceptance of suitable work when offered by that agency were the same as under the 1911 Act; nor was the machinery of Insurance Officer, Court of Referees, and Umpire altered, except that jurisdiction in questions of insurability was taken from the Umpire and vested in the Minister of Labor with right of appeal from him to a single Judge of the High Court, or of the Court of Session in Scotland. Two of the three important limitations (as apart from disqualifications) of the original Act were, however, changed as follows:

(1) The recipient of benefit must have paid at least twelve contributions in each insurance year, except that for the first year of operation four contributions were to entitle to a maximum of eight weeks' benefit (ten contributions without qualification were required under the 1914 Act).

(2) Payment of benefit was not intended to exceed fifteen weeks in the insurance year (as under the 1911 Act).

(3) Six weeks' contributions were established as the normal prerequisite for one week's benefit (five weeks' under the 1911 Act).

The similarity of the above limitations to those of the pre-war Acts showed a firm confidence in the stability of the old system, and a belief that once out-of-work donations could be dispensed with national unemployment insurance would again be built up as a reliable defense against the evils of unemployment. But the period of real test was still to come.

A little analysis indicates that this confidence in the old system permitted imitation to obscure good judgment. The 1911 Act had been launched at the beginning of a period of unusual prosperity, and its founders had been very careful not to predict success for the scheme during a period of depression inevitable at some future date. When the 1920 Act was drawn up, the state of Europe made it apparent that a severe slump in trade was likely to succeed the misleading activity which for a brief period followed the war. Nevertheless, entirely aside from the failure to take action during six fruitful years, the Act of 1920 committed two positive blunders which alone were sufficient to ensure failure. The first was in esti-mating the maximum unemployment which the Act would have to face as considerably less, even, than had the 1911 measure. A simple calculation will show that an average unemployment of five and one half per cent would soon, unless restrictions on the payment of benefit were enforced, have made expenditure more than revenue, and this degree of unemployment was reached before the Act had been a month in operation.

The second mistake was that, taking into consideration the reduced value of the currency, the scales of contri-butions and benefits, particularly the former, were actually lower, although nominally higher, than those in force before the war. And this in spite of the fact that the pre-war scales were admittedly too low to be of much use in periods of other than good employment. The table on page 38, showing the percentage increase in benefits and contributions when the new Act became operative over those in force in July, 1914, compared with the "increase in the cost of maintaining unchanged the pre-war (July,

1914) standard of living of the working classes" (Ministry of Labor statistics), will make this more plain.

TABLE III. PERCENTAGE INCREASE AT NOVEMBER, 1920, OVER JULY, 1914, OF COST OF LIVING, UNEMPLOYMENT BENEFITS, AND CONTRIBUTIONS

| LIVING COSTS | MAXIMUM BENEFIT | | STATE CONTRIBUTION IN RESPECT OF | | EMPLOYEE'S CONTRIBUTION | | EMPLOYER'S CONTRIBUTION IN RESPECT OF | |
|---|---|---|---|---|---|---|---|---|
| | Man | Woman | Man | Woman | Man | Woman | Man | Woman |
| 176%a | 114% | 71% | 20% | No increase | 60% | 20% | 60% | 40% |

a It is only fair to note that living costs reached their maximum in November, 1920. In August, 1920, when the Act was passed, they were 155 per cent above those of July, 1914. They did not fall below a 114 per cent increase until October, 1921.

In other respects the 1920 Act made a good deal of alteration in the body of previous unemployment insurance legislation. The entire group of measures designed to reduce unemployment by refunds was revised. In seven years the refunds to work-people with a long record of employment had amounted to less than £16,000, while refunds to employers in respect of work-people continuously employed had totaled £689,299. The first of these was renewed;[1] the second was not. These measures were so ingenious that in practice the difficulties and expense of operating them far out-weighed their possible benefit. In their secondary aspect of compromise measures designed to render the principle of compulsory insurance more palatable, it may be said that their effect was utterly negligible. The 1920 Act, however, still sought to discourage casual employment by a provision that, "where the employed person is employed by more than one person in any calendar week, the first person employing him in that week . . . shall be deemed to be the employer for the purposes . . . relating to the payment of con-

[1] The liability of the Unemployment Fund under the provision for refunds at the age of sixty naturally increased as time went on. During the insurance year 1922–23 it amounted to approximately £190,000. In April, 1924, legislation was brought forward to abolish these refunds for the future,

tributions." The rather futile effort to popularize the Exchanges with employers by having those agencies take over the clerical duties involved in the Act for employers who utilized them was also continued. Except in the special cases of the Liverpool Dock Scheme and the South Wales Ship Repairing Scheme this arrangement has fallen into desuetude, only four firms with 1700 employees making use of it in June, 1923.

By far the most important part of the 1920 Act, so far as building for the future is concerned, is found in the group of measures to be considered next — those encouraging voluntary unemployment insurance. These are of three distinct types: Arrangements with Associations of Employed Persons; Special Schemes; and Supplementary Schemes; the two last-named opening up a much broader vista than had been attempted by any previous legislation. Sections 18 to 21 (inclusive) of the Act, which explain the highly interesting Special and Supplementary Schemes, are given in full in Appendix II. Supplementary Schemes, under which an industry may levy additional contributions on its employers and employed in order to supplement the standard benefit, need no attention here. Up to the date of publication no action had been taken under this provision.

### Arrangements with Associations

The Arrangements with Associations of Employed Persons (Section 17) were based upon the similar provisions of the 1911 Act (cf. p. 16). There is, however, the important difference that, in addition to trade unions, societies "approved" under the Health Insurance Act of 1911 are encouraged to administer the payment of State unemployment insurance benefit, provided such a society has a system of ascertaining conditions of employment among its members and of obtaining notification of vacant posts for its members. Eligible societies are allowed to pay the State benefit direct to their members, recovering the sum periodically from the Insurance Fund. It was now laid down that, after an interim period (which with the advent of the depression was extended to October, 1924), the total benefit paid by the Association must exceed the benefit payable under the Act by at least one third in order to gain this privilege. The direct subventions to trade-union funds were abolished. This method of encouraging voluntary insurance no longer seemed necessary with by far the greater proportion of trade unionists compulsorily insured.

Social antagonisms were stimulated by the step which enabled approved societies other than trade unions to administer the payment of unemployment insurance benefit. On a smaller scale the development has caused much the same furor in British labor circles as the drive to establish "company unions" has stirred up in parallel quarters in America — and for much the same reason. By British trade unionists it is commonly regarded as an attempt to vest in the hands of employers' organizations that degree of control over the supply of labor which is implied in the administration of unemployment insurance. And there is much more than imagination in the labor argument that, with the control of administration in the hands of employers, regulations would gradually develop which would "seriously interfere with the right of workers to leave their employers, with their right to move about freely, with their right to strike." [1]

The Labor Party fight against Section 17 of the Act of 1920 was at the time based largely on the very justifiable stand that this step enabled provident associations only indirectly connected with industry to pay unemployment insurance benefits. This objection is no longer to the fore, for the good reason that many of the "Friendly Societies" have been unable to meet the provisions demanding that

[1] *Social Insurance and Trade Union Membership*, The Labor Joint Publications Dept., 1923, p. 18. See this pamphlet for the official Labor position on the issue.

such associations show means of ascertaining wages and conditions in all trades represented among their members, to say nothing of the requisite facilities for ascertaining and notifying vacancies. Of the 141 Associations, with an insured membership of about one million, with whom arrangements under Section 17 were still in force in July, 1923, only 23 Associations, with a membership of about 65,000, were not trade unions.

There remains, however, the administration of unem-
ployment insurance by a small number of individual firms acting in conjunction with the so-called National Federation of Employees' Approved Societies, generally known as the "Lesser" scheme after Mr. Henry Lesser, president of the N.F.E.A.S. While the members of each approved society affiliated with this federation are all drawn from the employees of a particular company or firm, thus weakening trade-union strength within that firm, the Federation itself is allied with the nation-wide Chambers of Commerce organization for purposes of vacancy notification. The endeavor to utilize the organization of Chambers of Commerce to set up privately operated Employment Exchanges competing with the State system is with justice suspected by British Labor as a step by the participating interests towards obtaining possession of the machinery of social insurance. As against this viewpoint, however, must be considered Mr. Lesser's reiterated statement that the scheme of the National Federation of Employees' Approved Societies for the administration of unemployment insurance in individual firms has "the ultimate object of its expansion and application to each organized industry as a separate, self-supporting entity." As will be discussed later, this objective is highly desirable in itself. But only if it is intended to give the trade unions as national organizations their full share of control — in steps towards the goal as well as when the goal is reached.

The original intention of this controversial section of the Act of 1920 appears to have been to forward possible amalgamation of the administration of national health insurance with that of unemployment insurance. It is to be remembered, however, that at bottom health insurance and unemployment insurance are in different categories. Major responsibility for the former properly rests upon the community. Major responsibility for the latter rests to a large extent upon industry.

SPECIAL SCHEMES

The Special Schemes are of supreme importance because they provide the means, originally intended to be applicable at any time, whereby unemployment insurance by industries may be substituted for unemployment insurance by the State. A "Special Scheme" is a draft plan for insurance by industry submitted to the Minister of Labor for approval. It must in the first instance be acceptable either to the Joint Industrial Council of the industry or to an "association of employers and employees" representing a substantial majority of each party. It asks permission to "contract out" of the system of State-controlled unemployment insurance altogether.

Where such a scheme came into force, the Government agreed to subsidize it annually up to a sum equivalent to three tenths of the State contribution which would have been paid, in the absence of such scheme, in respect of employed persons in the industry in question. While this subsidy, when calculated on the basis of the individual worker, seems very small, amounting (on the basis of the very low 1920 scale of State contribution) to 2s. 7½d. per man per annum and 2s. 2d. per woman per annum continuously employed, it is not so negligible when calculated in terms of the membership of an industry. In the case of the relatively small pottery industry, for instance, which in June, 1922, was estimated to have 70,060 workpeople, the proposed State subsidy would, if all the workers were continuously employed, amount to £8322 per annum under the 1920 scale of State contribution. While on the basis of the much higher State contribution laid down by the Unemployment Insurance Act of April, 1922,[1] the subsidy to the pottery industry alone might reach £27,000 per annum.

Two necessary conditions were laid down by the 1920 Act as prerequisites for establishing a scheme of insurance by industry. They were: (1) that the scheme should provide unemployment insurance either for all the employed persons in the industry, or for "all those persons other than any specified classes thereof"; and (2) that the benefits, whether for complete unemployment or systematic short-time, should not be less favorable than the benefits provided by the national system. With these statutory qualifications it was open to the Minister of Labor to approve any adequate special scheme submitted to him and in certain circumstances even to initiate such a scheme on his own responsibility, after appropriate consultation.

The provision for the establishment of insurance by industry was largely the result of a protracted agitation in' behalf of the principle of industrial maintenance, an idea behind the broad outline of which theorists with very different ultimate aims are able to combine effectively. A short track to insurance by industry had been marked out by the formation of the Whitley (Joint Industrial) Councils, and initial steps along this path whole-hearted supporters of the capitalist system and Guild Socialists could both approve.[2]   When the passage of the 1920 Act brought what had been an ideal well within the horizon of practical achievement, interest naturally redoubled. No time was lost in drawing up a number of schemes for contracting out of the State-operated system, the growing complexity and

---

[1] See p. 62.
[2] Lord Askwith and G. D. H. Cole, to mention only two of the well-known men of vastly different social viewpoint who are unanimous in urging industrial maintenance. See the evidence of the former before the Committee of Enquiry on Employment Exchanges (Cmd. 1140 (1921), pp. 81–93) and the pamphlet of the latter on *Unemployment and Industrial Maintenance*.

scope of which was viewed with increasing apprehension by those standing both to the right and to the left of State socialism.

In the middle of March, 1921, the *Labor Gazette* for that month reported that "the consideration of special schemes under Section 18 of the Unemployment Insurance Act, 1920, has been undertaken in all by thirteen Joint Industrial Councils, nine of whom have decided upon the preparation of special schemes. In one case the decision has since been rescinded; in five cases investigations are still in progress, and in three cases (wool, hosiery, and printing) schemes have now been drawn up, but have not yet been formally submitted to the Minister of Labor." While some of these schemes appear to have been insufficiently matured, the energy with which the study of insurance by industry was taken up in increasingly wider circles indicated that before many months active experimentation in this line would begin.

Such was the situation when progress in this direction was suddenly and effectively blocked. At the end of March, 1921, the percentage of unemployment among trade unions from which the Ministry of Labor receives regular returns stood at 10.0, having risen from 8.5 at the end of February, 6.9 at the end of January, and 6.0 at the end of December, 1920. On March 31, 1921, began the national stoppage of work in the coal mines, which, although the threatened triple alliance strike was averted, did not terminate until July 1st. Shortage of fuel quickly brought a number of the great coal-using industries nearly to a standstill, and this aggravation of an increase in unemployment, sufficiently disquieting by itself, quickly produced a most alarming situation. At the end of April, 1921, the trade-union percentage of unemployment, excluding coal-mining, stood at 17.6; at the end of May, 22.2; at the end of June, 23.1, a figure double that of any previous record in the preceding fifty years.[1]

[1] Some of the older trade unions carry their statistics of unemployment back to 1860. They have been published monthly in the

## ABROGATION OF SPECIAL SCHEMES

The Government insurance program, never too well prepared for any emergency, threatened to collapse completely under this strain, and in June, 1921, emergency legislation to save it was hastily rushed to Parliament. This panic-inspired Act [1] will be dealt with in its chronological position, but to round out the history of the schemes for insurance by industry it is necessary to quote one of its sections here. This section (number 5) read:

> The power of the Minister under section eighteen of the principal Act [that of 1920] to make special orders approving or making special schemes shall not be exercised during the deficiency period:
> Provided that this section shall not apply in any case where before the eighth day of June, nineteen hundred and twenty-one, a draft scheme appearing to the Minister to be complete has been submitted to him and application has, before that date, been made to him to approve the scheme in accordance with the provisions of section eighteen of the principal Act.

In January, 1921, the Unemployment Fund had shown a balance of £22,750,000, thanks to eight years of remarkably good employment and not to any special effort on the part of those in control to safeguard that reserve. In July, 1921, the surplus of the Fund was reduced to £100,000. On March 18, 1922, the outstanding debt of the Fund was nearly £14,000,000, at which time the Government Actuary estimated that by July, 1923, this debt might be swollen to £27,000,000.[2] However, gradual improvement in employment helped to check the increase. The debt reached a maximum of something over £17,000,000 in March, 1923. By the end of October, 1923, it had been reduced to £13,180,000.

With the national system unable to make ends meet the Government argued that, for the period of depression at

official *Labor Gazette* since 1893. The subject of trade union unemployment statistics is given full discussion in Chapter X.

[1] Unemployment Insurance (No. 2) Act, 1921.

[2] Report by Government Actuary under date of March 25, 1922 (Cmd. 1620, p. 5).

least, all hope of launching preparatory schemes of insurance by industry, even in the well-organized, stable trades, had vanished. With unemployment in several of the important industries ranging over twenty per cent for months at a time, it would have been impossible for either employers or workers in these hard-hit trades to pay contributions on the scale demanded by that rate of unemployment. Even had there been a State subsidy to spare, it was asserted, no special scheme launched without a tremendous financial reserve at a time of such widespread and extremely severe unemployment, could possibly have remained solvent. To withdraw industries with relatively little unemployment from the State-operated system would, it was claimed, be financially unfair to those affected above the average. And overlooking the difficulties of demarcation, inadequate labor and employers' organization, and kindred problems, there remained the fact that industrial bitterness was stimulated by the serious disputes which accompanied the depression period. Such an atmosphere is manifestly unfavorable to the establishment of a successful scheme of insurance by industry.[1]

One special scheme was, indeed, actually approved by special order of the Minister of Labor on June 24, 1921, and came into force on July 4th of that year.[2] It applied to the heterogeneous business of private insurance, or the "Insurance Industry" as this business has come to be technically known. Due attention to this interesting venture will be given in Chapter XI. To take it up here would unduly interrupt analysis of the operation of the national system during the depression period.

[1] The arguments of the opposition to insurance by industry are merely stated here. Their validity is examined in Chapter XI.

[2] A complete draft scheme of insurance by industry for the banking industry was submitted to the Ministry of Labor on June 7, 1921. But because of reasonable doubt as to whether the association submitting it represented a majority of the employees in this industry, it was held in abeyance for three years. On May 26, 1924, the Minister of Labor announced intention to approve this scheme, applicable to to the banking industry in England and Wales. (*Ministry of Labor Gazette*, June, 1924, p. 227.)

It should be noted, however, that the Insurance Industry is in many fundamentals of employment work in a class apart from ordinary productive industry. The industry is abnormally stable — its unemployment did not rise much above two per cent during the worst of the depression period. Its insured employees, with the exception of a relatively trivial proportion of messengers, janitors, and such, are almost exclusively clerical workers. The demarcation from other industries is exceptionally easy to draw. In this industry it has been possible to handle employment work without resorting to Employment Exchange machinery.

Nevertheless, as will be later pointed out,[1] the Insurance Industry experiment has been not only of intrinsic interest, but also a justification to those who believe that the principle of insurance by industry must gradually supplant the unwieldy system managed by the State.

We return to our consideration of the Government unemployment insurance program.

### FEATURES OF THE ACT OF 1920

Before taking up the emergency legislation which followed the Act of 1920, it will be useful briefly to analyze the main features of this last measure, passed on the threshold of the depression period. In Chapter II a summary of the 1911 Act was made under the five headings of Compulsion; Subvention; Contribution; Prevention; and Limitation. A similar summary for the 1920 Act will show most clearly the alterations accepted by the Government as advisable as a result of eight years' experience. The whole of this intervening period, it must be remembered, was one in which employment was exceptionally good; the alterations made, in other words, were deliberately chosen as advisable and not dictated by hostile circumstance.

COMPULSION. This principle was not only maintained, but its application was extended to three times the number

[1] See pp. 158–66.

of workers insured against unemployment by the State in 1916, and more than five times the number thus insured by the Act of 1911. Even before the war the introduction of compulsory insurance met with surprisingly little opposition from any responsible quarter, and war-time experience undoubtedly made its extension easier. As early as 1913, Professor Pigou had stated the opinion of many with regard to unemployment insurance by writing that "the unpopularity of compulsion appears to be imaginary rather than real, at all events among the work-people of Western Europe." [1] With an important qualification it may be said that time has vindicated this judgment. Compulsion, latent or exercised, is a law of civilization, and it is generally not the mere fact of compulsion which induces hostility, but the nature of the agency exercising this force. It is to be noted, therefore, that the Act of 1920 followed the demand of the times for recognition of personality by its provisions that compulsion might be exercised through democratic groups of kindred interest rather than by the impersonal Leviathan of the modern State.

SUBVENTION. Because the great majority of trade-union members were now compulsorily insured, the "Ghent system" of direct subvention to trade unions paying out-of-work benefit was abolished. It was replaced by the subsidy which the Government pledged itself to pay to the individual insurance funds of industries contracting out of the national scheme as units. The arrangements whereby trade unions paying unemployment benefit of their own were allowed to administer the payment of State benefits were continued, and even extended to include all "approved societies" with the necessary machinery of administration.

CONTRIBUTION. The scheme of triple contributions from State, employer, and worker was not altered. The argument has been advanced that the worker should be relieved of this burden, but the case for such a policy

[1] *Unemployment*, p. 227.

cannot be said to be proven. It is doubtful whether the average employer or employers' association is fundamentally any more responsible for unemployment than is the average trade unionist or trade union. The major causes of unemployment are deeper to seek, and the corollary sometimes drawn, that because the employee may not be responsible for losing his job, the employer necessarily is, is very often fallacious. A strike in such a basic industry as coal-mining will (whatever the justification for such action) by decision of the employees alone very rapidly create unemployment in other industries, strive the employers of those other industries how they may to avert it. Other arguments against canceling the workers' contribution will occur to the reader. It is certainly desirable that the workers should have a direct interest in the efficiency of operation if insurance by industry is to give them an equal share in control. Theoretically, at least, these contributions do something towards steadying expenditure over the trade cycle. But the further objection, sometimes raised, that to abolish the workers' contribution would make a system of unemployment insurance uncomfortably resemble one of doles, has little validity.[1] Of course these considerations do not mean that the workers' contribution should necessarily remain as large relatively to that of the employers as it has been in the past.

A more difficult question under the head of contribution was whether or not the rates of contribution in different industries should, as hitherto, continue to be the same. Unemployment has very different incidence on different

[1] For instance, under the Insurance Industry Special Scheme, employees' contributions have been abolished for seven years and will be reëstablished thereafter only if it is found that the employers' contributions alone are insufficient. This does not mean that the scheme is any the less one of insurance. A distinctive feature of social insurance is that only a part of the direct cost is paid by those receiving the benefits. A scheme in which none of the direct cost is paid by the beneficiary group does not for that reason cease to be entitled to the name "insurance." Because A pays the life insurance of B, the latter is none the less insured.

industries, and at a time of depression the percentage of unemployment may vary (as was the case in June, 1921) from 3.10 in one insured trade (tramway and omnibus service) to 63.39 in another (iron and steel manufacture). With such variations possible should contributions from all industries be uniform?

The decision took the line that a State-operated system cannot attempt to adjudicate between the risks of one industry and those of another, and that the system was quite complicated enough to handle without interfering with the uniformity of contributions. Incidentally, there seems no fundamental reason why the variation of unemployment risk between different industries should be considered any more than the equally important variation of risk between different ages.[1] It was, however, anticipated that industries with consistently low unemployment would be the first to take advantage of the contracting-out facilities in order to work out in their own behalf a more scientific system of contributions. And there is no doubt that the crudity of the State-operated system in this respect is an argument in favor of insurance by industry. As is pointed out on pages 153–54 the risk could as readily be spread over the whole field of industry on this basis.

PREVENTION. As has been noted, the refund system of the 1911 Act was in 1920 swept away, with the single exception of repayments to work-people reaching the age of sixty with a long record of contributions. These plans to reduce unemployment were found in practice to complicate operation without achieving their object in any noticeable degree. The regulations for casual employment of the 1920 Act, amounting in effect to a small fine for the employer who engages labor for a period of less than a week's duration, require little additional clerical effort, but have proved almost equally ineffective for the object sought. Experience with this type of petty measure has

---

[1] See an article by the author on "The Incidence of Unemployment by Age and Sex," in the *Economic Journal* of December, 1922.

proved its utter inadequacy as a factor in the prevention of unemployment. He is a rare employer who will retain a man whom he would otherwise discharge in order to claim at the end of a year one third of the few shillings' contribution he has made to the insurance fund in respect of that man. Nor will a shipping company give orders to employ the same docker six days a week merely because they must pay a week's insurance contribution if they only employ him one day. Coupled with more far-reaching measures these experiments might have utility commensurate with the complications which they involve. Alone they are like pin pricks which antagonize the employer without securing his coöperation for the objects sought.

LIMITATION. The limitations on the payment of benefit were kept substantially the same as under the 1911 Act. So long as employment continued abnormally good, they served their purpose. The seeds of trouble lay not with the safeguards, but with the totally inadequate benefit which they safeguarded. As the necessity for instituting out-of-work donation after the Armistice had indicated, while the fortifications were sound the fort was mined within. This was to be shown very early in the depression which followed on the heels of the inauguration of the Act of 1920.

# CHAPTER V

## THE DEGENERATION OF STATE-OPERATED UN-EMPLOYMENT INSURANCE

HITHERTO, although necessarily somewhat complicated, an analytical survey of the development of the State-operated unemployment insurance system has been a relatively straightforward matter. The period 1911 to 1920 was one of very decided progress in this field of socialistic enterprise. The legislative alterations, put through under favorable circumstances, brought changes which experience had indicated would improve the operation and strengthen the defenses of the program.

It now becomes necessary to turn to the record of rapid degeneration which overtook the system of unemployment insurance with the advent of the post-war depression. The facts of this degeneration are questioned by none, although excused by many. Whether or not these facts are in themselves an indictment of the principle on which unemployment insurance has hitherto been operated in Great Britain will be discussed in the chapter which follows this.

All unemployment insurance legislation in the twenty-eight months of depression between the inauguration of the Act of 1920 and the inauguration of the Act of March, 1923, was run up because of the necessities of the moment, and not, as most of the legislation previously considered, planned for permanency. In consequence it is unnecessary to give the decline period of the system the same sort of analysis as was essential for the earlier Acts. The design of this chapter is self-determined — merely to point out the important alterations brought by each of this last series of Acts. Except as a warning there is in them little to warrant the attention of the student of unemployment insurance or of unemployment relief in general.

## THE ACT OF MARCH, 1921

The Unemployment Insurance Act, 1921 — the first important measure after the 1920 Act [1] — was enacted on March 3, 1921, and came into operation the same day. It altered the parent Act (that of 1920) in two directions: by increasing the amount of benefit and contributions, and by lowering the limitations on the payment of benefit. Weekly contributions [2] and maximum weekly benefit were established as follows:

|  | MEN | WOMEN | BOYS | GIRLS |
|---|---|---|---|---|
|  |  |  | (16 and 17 years of age) | |
| State contribution . . | 2.75d. | 2.25d. | 1.375d. | 1.125d. |
| Employed person . . | 5d. | 4d. | 2.5d. | 2d. |
| Employer . . . . . . | 6d. | 5d. | 3d. | 2.5d. |
| Total contribution in respect of individual . . . . | 1s. 1.75d. | 11.25d. | 6.875d. | 5.625d. |
| Maximum benefit . . | 20s. | 16s. | 10s. | 8s. |

The really significant alterations of the Act were those affecting limitations on the payment of benefit. It will be remembered that under the Act of 1920 the three principal limitations were:

(1) Six weeks of contribution for one week of benefit.

(2) Not more than fifteen weeks of benefit a year.

(3) Eligibility to depend on the payment of twelve contributions a year.

All three of these limitations were (not four months after the 1920 Act began to operate) swept away for those normally engaged in insurable employment who were through no fault of their own unable to meet the existing require-

[1] A temporary Act passed December 23, 1920, made eligible for benefit large numbers of work-people who had been unemployed when the Act of 1920 came into force. Its only importance lies in the fact that by allowing eight weeks of benefit without contribution it inaugurated the principle of "uncovenanted benefit" which was to wreck the insurance program.

[2] As the contributions were not to be increased until July 4, 1921, by which date another scale was in effect, their interest is somewhat theoretical!

ments. In their place were established the following provisions:

## UNCOVENANTED BENEFIT

(1) During a period of sixteen months, thirty-two weeks of benefit were to be allowed, with the provision that no more than sixteen of them might be drawn in each of two "special periods" of eight months' duration. The first special period ran from March 3 to November 2, 1921; the second special period was to have run [1] from November 3, 1921, to July 2, 1922. Thus a rate of twenty-four weeks of benefit a year was established for the former fifteen weeks.

(2) Instead of the payment of a certain number of contributions a year, the principal preliminary qualification for the receipt of benefit was made proof of twenty weeks' employment since December 31, 1919. In the case of ex-service men the necessary period of proved employment was reduced to ten weeks, with the provision that in special cases it might be waived altogether. This limitation naturally became less and less rigid as December 31, 1919, receded further into the past. Benefit paid under this qualification was known as "uncovenanted benefit," in contradistinction to that credited under the statutory limitations of the 1920 Act (see p. 36). While most of these requirements were still technically maintained, none were excluded from benefit under the depression period Acts for being unable to meet them. Thus covenanted and uncovenanted benefit went on side by side, the proportion of the latter increasing as time passed. Uncovenanted benefit has been, however, refused to certain classes of aliens, to single persons able to obtain support through relatives and to those who refuse work to which they may not be used but which they are "reasonably capable of performing." Benefit of this type was, strictly speaking, a discretionary grant by the Minister of Labor. But under the regularized limitations it was actually given or withheld by

[1] "Was to have run" because a third special period had to be started when the second was little more than half expired. See p. 59.

decision of the Local Employment Committees, unpaid volunteer bodies whose position in the system is explained in Chapter VIII.

In addition the Act of March, 1921, provided that advances up to ten million pounds might be obtained from the Treasury in order to maintain the Fund in solvency, as against the limit of three million pounds under the 1911 Act. With regard to the arrangements with associations of insured persons under the 1920 Act, the provision was laid down that the benefits of such associations must exceed the State benefit not by one third but by 5s., 4s., 2s. 6d., and 2s. per week in the case of men, women, boys, and girls respectively.

The above Act had been based on the assumption that the rate of unemployment would not exceed an average of 9.5 per cent for the sixteen months (ending July, 1922) which were covered by its special periods.[1] Since, when the measure was introduced in Parliament, on February 21, 1921, the percentage of unemployment among insured work-people already stood at this figure, and was rising rapidly, it would seem that the assumption was optimistic, to say the least. The effects of the national stoppage in the coal-mining industry aggravated the rate of increase, and by the end of May, 1921, the percentage of unemployment among insured work-people had risen to 17.3.[2] Benefit was being paid out at the rate of £2,000,000 a week against a total income from contributions of under £350,000 a week. The depression had not lasted eight months, but already immediate insolvency threatened the national unemployment insurance system. New legislation had to be hurriedly drawn up, was introduced in the House of Commons on June 8th, and rushed through under the plea of vital urgency. On July 1st, the Unemployment Insurance

[1] *Labor Gazette*, June, 1921, p. 282.
[2] Excluding miners who had voluntarily ceased work. In Chapter X will be found a full explanation of the differences between the Trade Union and Insured Trades percentages of unemployment.

(No. 2) Act of 1921 was passed, certain of its provisions being made to come into operation a day before passage.

## THE ACT OF JULY, 1921

The measures taken by this Act were of conflicting purpose. On the one hand, an effort was made to meet the financial difficulty by again raising the scale of contributions, while restoring benefits to the level of the 1920 Act. On the other hand, limitations on the payment of benefit were lowered still further in an effort to meet the predicament of the unemployed who had in the first four months of the first special period exhausted most of the sixteen weeks' benefit supposed to last them for eight months. As it was obvious that the effect of the first of these measures, making for solvency, would not outweigh the effect of the second, making for insolvency, the amount which might be borrowed from the Treasury was raised from ten million to twenty million pounds.

The new scale of weekly contributions and benefit was:

| | MEN | WOMEN | BOYS | GIRLS |
| --- | --- | --- | --- | --- |
| | | | (16 and 17 years of age) | |
| State contribution . . | 3.75d. | 3.25d. | 1.875d. | 1.625d. |
| Employed person . . | 7d. | 6d. | 3.5d. | 3d. |
| Employer . . . . . . | 8d. | 7d. | 4d. | 3.5d. |
| Total contribution in respect of individual . . . | 1s. 6.75d. | 1s. 4.25d. | 9.375d. | 8.125d. |
| Maximum benefit . . | 15s. | 12s. | 7s. 6d. | 6s. |

The period in which an unemployed worker in an insured trade could draw benefit was increased still further by adding six weeks to each of the special periods of sixteen weeks established by the preceding Act. This made possible forty-four weeks of benefit in sixteen months, or a rate of thirty-three weeks a year. It will be seen that in respect of an insured workman who drew the maximum benefit to which he was entitled under this Act, the State would, in a year, pay out £24.15.0 in benefit (33 × 15s.) while receiving from him and his employer as contributions to the

Fund a maximum of only £1.3.9 (19 × 1s. 3d.). Therefore, in respect of an unemployed man drawing full benefit an outright dole of 14s. 3d. a week for thirty-three weeks a year could have been substituted for the insurance benefit of 15s. without costing the State a penny extra. On financial grounds, in other words, there was little to choose between unemployment insurance for those beginning to draw full uncovenanted benefit and a system of highly regularized State subsidy to the unemployed.

Still less was there to choose, as we shall see, when the Act of April, 1922, by curtailing the duration of the second special period, raised the actual (as opposed to scheduled) period of benefit for the fifty-seven weeks March 3, 1921, to April 5, 1922, to forty-four weeks, or a rate of forty weeks per year.

Reference has already been made [1] to the section of this Act which suspended the initiation of special schemes of unemployment insurance for particular industries. In June, 1921, when the effect of the prolonged stoppage of work in the mining industry was added to the effects of the general trade depression, unemployment reached a stage without precedent in the history of Great Britain. On June 24, 1921, out of 12,190,740 insured work-people, 2,171,288 were registered at the Employment Exchanges as out of work, in addition to 833,000 who were working systematic short-time in such a manner as to entitle them to claim to benefit. In hardly any major industry was there less than ten per cent of unemployment at this time, while in a number of important industries the proportion of employees out of work was more than one third. When the large amount of unsystematized short-time and the smaller proportion of short-time so arranged by employers as to entitle benefit are taken into account, it is probable that underemployment was at this and subsequent periods approximately half as considerable as complete unemployment. At the end of June, 1921, in other words,

[1] See p. 45.

a full quarter of the labor power of Great Britain was involuntarily idle.[1] Under these conditions no major industry could hope to make a start in carrying the burden of its own unemployment.

## UNEMPLOYED WORKERS' DEPENDANTS ACT

The Unemployed Workers' Dependants (Temporary Provision) Act which was passed by Parliament on November 8, 1921, caused the third alteration of the year in the unemployment insurance program. Although not itself an insurance measure in any strict sense of the term, being designed "to make temporary provision for the payment of grants to unemployed workers towards the maintenance of their wives, dependent husbands, and dependent children," it was operated through the machinery of the insurance Acts and was later (by the Act of April, 1922) formally amalgamated with them.

Under it special grants for dependants were allowed unemployed workers in receipt of unemployment benefit under the Acts of 1920 and 1921. Those who established claim to these grants received them weekly together with their unemployment benefit, and the extra contributions entailed for employers and employed persons were added to the regular insurance contributions, a single stamp representing the combined value being affixed to the Unemployment Books. Grants were allowed, with adequate safeguards, at the rate of 5s. per week for a wife or invalid husband, and at the rate of 1s. per week for each dependent child. A grant was not allowed in respect of a wife herself in receipt of State unemployment benefit, or who "is in regular wage-earning employment or is engaged in any business or other occupation ordinarily carried on for profit." The weekly rates of extra contributions for the

[1] See *The Third Winter of Unemployment*, pp. 26–30. It is there estimated that even in September, 1922, "one fifth, or rather more of the national labor power (other than agriculture) was running to waste."

purpose of this Act, payable by all insured work-people and
not only those entitled to Dependants' Grants, were as
follows:

| | MEN | WOMEN | BOYS | GIRLS |
| --- | --- | --- | --- | --- |
| | | | (16 and 17 years of age) | |
| State contribution . . | 3d. | 2d. | 2d. | 2d. |
| Employed person . . | 2d. | 1d. | 1d. | 1d. |
| Employer . . . . . . | 2d. | 1d. | 1d. | 1d. |

As all insured persons and their employers, as well as
the State, had to contribute additionally to provide the
money for Dependants' Grants, the effect was to raise
more money than was expended for this purpose, and
therefore to check somewhat the alarming financial drain.
During the period November, 1921, to April, 1922, of the
total work-peoples' and employers' contributions, £2,600-
000; of the State contribution, £2,100,000; and of the total
benefits paid out, £3,590,000 were in respect of Dependants' Grants. The effect of this Act while a temporary
measure was, therefore, to provide a bonus of £1,110,000
for the Unemployment Fund.

Unemployment continuing with but little abatement
during the early months of 1922, two factors caused the
Ministry of Labor before the end of April again to revise
the insurance code. One was that the sixteen weeks of
benefit originally allowed for the second special period
(November 3, 1921, to July 2, 1922), even as increased to
twenty-two weeks by the second Unemployment Insurance
Act of 1921, had turned out to be insufficient. The solution
found for this difficulty was simply to establish a third
special period, beginning in the middle of the second, for
which, of course, new legislation was required. The second
factor was the temporary nature of the Unemployed Workers' Dependants' Act, which was scheduled to end on May
9, 1922. Further legislation was required if the grants
which it carried were not to be discontinued. The solution
found for this difficulty was officially to amalgamate these
grants as part of the permanent unemployment insurance

program for as long as the period of deficiency on the Unemployment Fund continued.

CONTINUOUS BENEFIT UNDER UNEMPLOYMENT INSURANCE

Far more important than any of the provisions of the Act of April, 1922, is the fact that by it the Ministry of Labor accepted the principle of continuous benefit, thereby turning unemployment insurance into a system in fundamentals indistinguishable from one of State doles. The third special period established by this Act went into effect on April 6, 1922, and the second special period was brought to a close on the day preceding. From November 3, 1921, when it began, to April 5, 1922, when it terminated, was a period of exactly twenty-two calendar weeks and in this period twenty-two weeks of benefit were payable with practically no requirements as to the contributions which made the system one of insurance. In that fact, which because of the maze of legislation surrounding it was realized by hardly anyone outside of the Ministry of Labor, is found conclusive proof that State-operated unemployment insurance in Great Britain had collapsed under the strain of the depression period. For many who were still nominally "insured" against unemployment the system of relief had ceased to be one of insurance. To call by that name a system of relief in which continuous benefit is paid out without any reference to contributions paid in, is to juggle words to the verge of conscious deception.[1]

There is evidence available of the extent to which uncovenanted benefit, when the depression period was well advanced, replaced that drawn as of right by virtue of contributions. On January 27, 1923, the Ministry of Labor collected for detailed analysis a sample of over 370,000 claims to unemployment benefit current in Great Britain

[1] Palpably misleading is the official statement in the *Report on National Unemployment Insurance to July, 1923* (p. 9) that "benefit has never been payable continuously to persons unemployed for very long periods."

on that day. This was about thirty per cent of the total number of claims current at Employment Exchanges on the date mentioned, and as the Ministry of Labor observed: "The results of the analysis may with some confidence be regarded as applicable to the whole number of claims." [1]

As at the time of the inquiry thirty weeks had elapsed since the beginning (July 1, 1922) of the insurance year then current, a maximum of thirty insurance contributions was possible in each individual Unemployment Book. Yet 38.2 per cent of the 302,829 adult male claims analyzed and 25.6 per cent of the 58,923 adult female claims analyzed showed no contributions at all paid in those thirty weeks. In other words, something over one third of all adult benefit claimants at this time had paid no contributions at all in the insurance year, although seven months of that year had elapsed. It should perhaps be noted that disabled ex-service men, of whom 13,622 were covered by the inquiry, raised somewhat the proportion of males without contributions to their credit.

Frequently the proportion of uncovenanted benefit granted rose much higher than one third. On October 9, 1922, for instance, 73.6 per cent of the current claims to benefit were of the uncovenanted type. Between November 8, 1920 and June 30, 1923, about £128,304,000 was paid out in unemployment benefit and Dependants' Grants. Of this total it is admitted by the Ministry of Labor that the proportion paid as uncovenanted benefit "may safely be put at more than one half." [2]

## THE ACT OF APRIL, 1922

The provisions of this Act, which was passed by Parliament on April 12, 1922, but made operative from April 6, 1922, may be briefly dismissed. As already observed, it amalgamated the rates of contribution under the Un-

[1] A detailed report on this interesting analysis is found in the *Labor Gazette*, November, 1923, pp. 395–396.

[2] *Report on National Unemployment Insurance to July, 1923*, p. 12.

employed Workers' Dependants' Act with those of the preceding Unemployment Insurance Act, the new scale of weekly contributions and benefit being:

|  | MEN | WOMEN | BOYS | GIRLS |
|---|---|---|---|---|
|  |  |  | (16 and 17 years of age) | |
| State contribution . . | 6.75$d$. | 5.25$d$. | 3.875$d$. | 3.625$d$. |
| Employed person . . | 9$d$. | 7$d$. | 4.5$d$. | 4$d$. |
| Employer . . . . . | 10$d$. | 8$d$. | 5$d$. | 4.5$d$. |
| Total contribution in respect of individual | 2s. 1.75$d$. | 1s. 8.25$d$. | 1s. 1.375$d$. | 1s. 0.125$d$. |
| Maximum benefit . . | 15s.* | 12s.* | 7s. 6d.* | 6s.* |

* Plus grants at the rate of 5s. per week for a wife or invalid husband, and 1s. per week for each dependent child.

Two new special periods of "uncovenanted benefit" were established, the third running from April 6, 1922,[1] to November 1, 1922, and the fourth from November 2, 1922, to July 1, 1923. During the third special period fifteen weeks' benefit were to be allowed, this, in the case of uncovenanted benefit, being payable in five-week periods with an interval or "gap" of five weeks after each benefit period. During the fourth special period twelve weeks of benefit were to be allowed, but authority was given to extend this twelve weeks to a maximum period of twenty-two weeks, subject to the claimant having three unexhausted contributions, whether old or recent, for each week of benefit over twelve weeks granted. This, it will be seen, made possible thirty-seven weeks of benefit in a period of sixty-four weeks, or a rate of 29.8 weeks of benefit a year. On paper this was a slight improvement on the provisions of the 1921 (No. 2) Act which had allowed benefit at a rate of thirty-three weeks a year.

But just as in practice the scheduled rate of thirty-three weeks' benefit per year had been increased to an actual rate of forty weeks' benefit by the patchwork method of

[1] Nothing shows better the plane to which State-operated unemployment insurance had sunk than this decision to make the Act become operative six days before it was passed by Parliament. Cf. what is said of the effect of this policy on Employment Exchange operation on pp. 123 to 125.

passing a new Act before the periods established by its predecessor had expired, so the Act of April, 1922, in its turn had soon to be subjected to more tinkering. On July 20, 1922, the Unemployment Insurance (No. 2) Act of 1922 was pushed through Parliament, allowing in the third special period twenty-two weeks of benefit instead of the fifteen weeks authorized three months previously. The rate of benefit was thereby increased to 35.75 weeks a year.

By means of this revising Act the Government struggled through the third special period. But four months after the fourth special period commenced, yet another Unemployment Insurance Act had to be drafted and taken through Parliament, most of the members, as their speeches or more eloquent silence indicated, having by this time lost all track of the tangles, problems, and subterfuges in which State-operated unemployment insurance was hopelessly involved.

The new Act provided that the fourth special period should run from November 2, 1922, to October 17, 1923, instead of to July 1, 1923, as originally planned. By allowing forty-four weeks of uncovenanted benefit in this new special period of fifty weeks' duration (that is, benefit at the rate of forty-six weeks a year), this Act of March, 1923, came closer to legalizing outright doles openly than any of its predecessors. All sense of stability had been swept out of the insurance program. The evidence was complete that these Acts of the depression period must not be judged by their provisions, but by the even more erratic alterations in those provisions brought about by the next opportunist measure.

But we outrun our chronological analysis.

"Uncovenanted benefit," the Act of April, 1922, provided further, would be granted to the extent outlined on page 62 whenever it was held "expedient in the public interest," the only qualification beside proofs of genuine desire for employment and normal membership in an insured trade on the part of the applicant, being: "*either* that not less than twenty contributions have been paid in respect of him under the principal Act (that of 1920), *or* that he has since December 31, 1919, been employed for a reasonable length of time in employment insurable under the 1920 Act." In the case of ex-service men, however, even this last provision might be waived.

The only other provision of the Act of April, 1922, which needs attention is that which raised the amount which might be borrowed from the Treasury to discharge liabilities of the Unemployment Fund from twenty million to thirty million pounds.

### THE ACT OF JULY, 1922

To round out this survey, the provisions of the Acts of July, 1922, and March, 1923, must be briefly summarized. That of July, 1922, besides increasing the number of weeks in the third special period from fifteen to twenty-two, also cut down the "gap" in uncovenanted benefit from five weeks to one week. Before a single gap of five weeks had been passed through, the Government had realized, as will be made clear in the next chapter, that such restrictions on the payment of benefit only resulted in throwing on local relief agencies the burden of supporting those debarred from the insurance fund. It therefore decided to take a further step in turning "benefits" into doles by reducing the enforced interval between the five-week benefit periods to a single week. In the debate preceding the passage of the Unemployment Insurance (No. 2) Act of 1922, the Labor Party endeavored to abolish the gap altogether, a step which would, of course, have definitely ended the pretense that the system of relief was still one of unemployment insurance. The Labor Party amendment, moved by Arthur Hayday and supported by J. R. Clynes and other Labor leaders, was, however, defeated, and eighteen months had to elapse before this party was able to press home its campaign to end gap periods.

The reduction of the "gap" period and the increase in the number of weeks of benefit allowed were the only changes made by the Act of July, 1922.

The Act of March, 1923 (Unemployment Insurance Act, 1923) was the only one of its kind that year and the last with which this study is intimately concerned. With the evidence presented in subsequent chapters it completes the case argued herein — that State-operated unemployment insurance proved not only an inadequate but also an impossible method of defense against unemployment during a period of severe depression.

## THE ACT OF MARCH, 1923

The provision of this measure authorizing a maximum of forty-four weeks' benefit in the fourth special period of fifty weeks has already been mentioned. It remains to be noted that the Act sought to hold to a faint shadow of the principles of insurance by providing that this forty-four weeks of uncovenanted benefit should be divided into two periods of twenty-two weeks each, separated by a "gap period" of two weeks in which benefit was refused.

No alteration in the rates of contribution and benefit was made, except that this Act made permanent the additional contributions and benefits payable in respect of dependants, which by increasing income more than expenditure had been instrumental in checking the rapid accumulation of deficit prior to their inception.[1]

Beginning in 1923, this Act altered the insurance year so as to run from mid-October to mid-October, and proposed that in the first year of this alteration (October, 1923, to October, 1924) "Twenty-six weeks of benefit may be paid, either in respect of contributions or, if necessary, irrespective of the payment of contributions." In uncovenanted benefit, however, it sought to maintain the

[1] The Act of April, 1922, had provided that the provisions for dependents should continue only until the end of the "deficiency period" of the Unemployment Fund.

"gap" principle by stipulating for a break of three weeks after payment of twelve weeks' benefit.[1] Abolition of the "gap" in February, 1924, was quickly followed by an Act, dated April 15, 1924, substituting a maximum of forty-one weeks of benefit for the twenty-six originally provided. Comment on this additional proof of insurance degeneration would be superfluous.

The Act of March, 1923, also proposed that after the end of the deficiency period the rates of contribution should be lowered. The maximum rates suggested were six pence a week from the employed person and six pence from the employer, in the case of a man; four pence from the employed person and five pence from the employer, in the case of a woman; and half these rates in the case of a boy or girl respectively. The State contribution after the end of the deficiency period was also to be reduced to one quarter of the joint contributions of employer and employed, instead of the proportion of approximately one third established by the Act of April, 1922. But small reliance could be placed on these provisions of an "insurance" program which had become as variable as the English climate.[2]

[1] In his initial speech as Premier in the House of Commons, Mr. J. Ramsay MacDonald, on February 12, 1924, announced the intention of the Government to abolish the "gap period" altogether, and hinted that it would be the policy of the Labor Government to eliminate the discretionary feature in the granting of uncovenanted benefit. He prefaced his remarks on this subject with the appropriate phrase: "doles or insurance." Except verbally the distinction had all but ceased to exist. When, a few days later, the Labor Government made elimination of the "gap period" the subject of its first legislative proposals there was little opposition from any quarter.

[2] Legislation introduced by the Labor Government in April, 1924, contemporaneously with the brief Act referred to in the text above, provided, among other changes, for (1) insurance of boys and girls between the ages of fourteen and sixteen; (2) increase in adult weekly rates of benefit to 18s. for men and 15s. for women, and doubling the 1s. a week allowance for each dependent child; (3) raising of the ratio of the State contribution after the end of the deficiency period to one half of the combined contributions of employers and employed as established by the Act of March, 1923. In connection with these proposals the Government Actuary estimated that the deficiency period would come to an end about June, 1926.

The history of twelve years of unemployment insurance legislation in Great Britain is now set forth. No such survey which aspires to thoroughness can avoid being confusing by reason of the great complexity and experimental or panic-stricken character of most of the measures. To simplify the task of the reader so far as possible the table on pp. 68-9 has been constructed, which, while making no pretense to cover all of the provisions of the various Acts, will furnish at a glance an impression of the principal changes wrought in State-operated unemployment insurance in Great Britain from its inception to the end of 1923.

### INSURANCE IN THEORY; DOLES IN FACT

A close analysis of the whole story has been necessary to indicate the full extent of degeneration. To one who has only followed the decline period from month to month, from measure to measure, insight into essentials will have been denied. The Ministry of Labor struggled hard to maintain the appearance of insurance during the depression period. The "special periods" of benefit were introduced as periods of emergency benefit, to be dispensed with at the earliest possible opportunity. The distinctive term of "uncovenanted benefit," applied to benefit allowed during these periods, indicates the underlying hope that such benefit, granted as a concession to unprecedented conditions, would be abolished as soon as the conditions which necessitated it were past. It was not in fact, but in theory, that unemployment insurance during the depression period differed from a highly regularized system of doles. Doles, disguised as "uncovenanted benefit" were allowed, but not as a settled policy.

It was this resolute adherence to the spirit of unemployment insurance, concealing a progressive surrender of its principles, which caused a widespread failure to appreciate the extent of the change which came over British unemployment relief policy during the post-war depression.

TABLE IV. SUMMARY OF THE UNEMPLOYMENT INSURANCE ACTS, 1911–23

| Act | Approximate Number Insured | Tri-partite Weekly Contribution in Respect of Individual Adult | | | | Maximum Weekly Benefit for Adult | | | | Maximum Advance from Treasury | Principal Limitations on Payment of Benefit[1] |
|---|---|---|---|---|---|---|---|---|---|---|---|
| | | Man s. | Man d. | Woman s. | Woman d. | Man s. | Man d. | Woman s. | Woman d. | £ | |
| (1) 1911 | 2,250,000 | — | 6.67 | — | 6.67 | 7 | — | 7 | — | 3,000,000 | (a) Not more than 15 weeks' benefit in 52. (b) Five weeks of contribution for one week of benefit. (c) Minimum of 26 weeks' employment in preceding 5 years. |
| (2) 1914 | As under 1 | As under 1 | | As under 1 | | As under 1 | | As under 1 | | As under 1 | (a) As under 1. (b) As under 1. (c) Minimum of 10 contributions required. |
| (3) 1916 | 4,000,000 | As under 1 | | As under 1 | | As under 1 | | As under 1 | | As under 1 | (a) As under 2. (b) As under 2. (c) As under 2. |
| (4) 1919 | As under 3 | As under 1 | | As under 1 | | 11 | — | 11 | — | As under 1 | (a) As under 2. (b) As under 2. (c) As under 2. |
| (5) 1920 | 12,000,000 | — | 10 | — | 8.17 | 15 | — | 12 | — | As under 1 | (a) As under 2. (b) Six weeks of contribution for one week of benefit. (c) Minimum of 12 contributions in an insurance year required. |
| (6) 1921 (March) | As under 5 | 1 | 1.75 | — | 11.25 | 20 | — | 16 | — | 10,000,000 | (a) Not more than 24 weeks' benefit in 52. (b) Abolished. (c) Minimum of 20 weeks' employment since Dec. 31, 1919 (10 weeks for ex-service men). |

1 Other than those designed to test reality of involuntary unemployment.

TABLE IV.  SUMMARY OF THE UNEMPLOYMENT INSURANCE ACTS, 1911–23—*Continued*

| ACT | APPROXIMATE NUMBER INSURED | TRI-PARTITE WEEKLY CONTRIBUTION IN RESPECT OF INDIVIDUAL ADULT | | MAXIMUM WEEKLY BENEFIT FOR ADULT | | MAXIMUM ADVANCE FROM TREASURY £ | PRINCIPAL LIMITATIONS ON PAYMENT OF BENEFIT |
|---|---|---|---|---|---|---|---|
| | | Man S. D. | Woman S. D. | Man S. D. | Woman S. D. | | |
| (7) 1921 (July) | As under 5 | 1   6.75 | 1   4.25 | 15   — | 12   — | 20,000,000 | (a) Not more than 33 weeks' benefit in 52. (c) As under 6. |
| (8) 1922 (April) | As under 5 | 2   1.75 | 1   8.25 | 15   —[1] | 12   —[1] | 30,000,000 | (a) Not more than 29.8 weeks' benefit in 52. (c) Employment for "a reasonable length of time" since Dec. 31, 1919, required (waivable for ex-service men). (d) Five weeks' gap between periods of uncovenanted benefit. |
| (9) 1922 (July) | As under 5 | As under 8 | As under 8 | As under 8 | As under 8 | As under 8 | (a) Not more than 35.75 weeks' benefit in 52. (c) As under 8. (d) Gap of one week between periods of uncovenanted benefit. |
| (10) 1923 (March) | As under 5 | As under 8 | As under 8 | As under 8 | As under 8 | As under 8 | (a) Not more than 46 weeks' benefit in 52. (c) As under 8. (d) Gap of two weeks between periods of uncovenanted benefit. |

[1] Plus Dependants' Grants.

The principle of insurance having been abandoned by degrees, never admittedly and always with the intention of restoration, there resulted a natural obscuration of the fact that much of the relief given as insurance had a much closer affinity to doles. Thus, in October, 1921, just before the start of the "second special period," which, as shown, gave twenty-two weeks' uncovenanted benefit for twenty-two weeks of unemployment, the official journal of the Ministry of Labor[1] prefaced an article on "Unemployment Relief" in Germany with the observation that "in the absence of a national system of unemployment insurance, donations to persons out of work in Germany are strongly suggestive of poor relief." This chapter should have made it obvious that during the depression period donations to persons out of work in England were to a large extent of exactly the same character in spite of a national system of unemployment insurance.

As trade revives, the heavy debt contracted by the Unemployment Fund will be paid off, and it is to be assumed that State-operated unemployment insurance will, as the industrial position improves, gradually again become insurance in fact as well as in name. But this will not alter the fact that as early in the depression as April, 1922, when continuous benefit had been (although not admittedly) operated through unemployment insurance machinery, it had been found advisable to adopt a system of disguised doles.

Such was the actual happening. In the next chapter attempt will be made to inquire into the inevitability of the collapse. For until the circumstances and possible alternatives to the course actually taken have been considered, an opinion that the degeneration can be regarded as an indictment of the principle on which unemployment insurance has hitherto been operated, would be premature.

[1] *Labor Gazette*, October, 1921, p. 523.

# CHAPTER VI

## INDICTMENTS FROM THE DEPRESSION PERIOD

NOTHING inspires misleading conclusions more readily than a mere record of the legislation of abnormal times, set out without reference to formative conditions. Supplementing what has already been said on the subject, it is therefore advisable again to emphasize the magnitude of the problem with which the State unemployment relief program was confronted from the autumn of 1920. This can be done clearly and briefly by a study of the following table and chart, compiled from Ministry of Labor statistics. The table shows the annual fluctuations in the percentage of unemployment among those trade unions making returns to the Ministry of Labor, from the beginning of the present century up to 1924. The chart carries these statistics back to the year 1874 and presents the whole material graphically.[1]

TABLE V.  FLUCTUATIONS IN TRADE-UNION UNEMPLOYMENT, 1900–24

(The annual percentage is the mean of twelve monthly percentages)

| YEAR | PERCENTAGE UNEMPLOYED | YEAR | PERCENTAGE UNEMPLOYED | YEAR | PERCENTAGE UNEMPLOYED |
|---|---|---|---|---|---|
| 1900 | 2.5 | 1908 | 7.8 | 1916 | 0.4 |
| 1901 | 3.3 | 1909 | 7.7 | 1917 | 0.7 |
| 1902 | 4.0 | 1910 | 4.7 | 1918 | 0.8 |
| 1903 | 4.7 | 1911 | 3.0 | 1919 | 2.4 |
| 1904 | 6.0 | 1912 | 3.2 | 1920 | 2.4 |
| 1905 | 5.0 | 1913 | 2.1 | 1921 | 15.3 |
| 1906 | 3.6 | 1914 | 3.3 | 1922 | 15.4 |
| 1907 | 3.7 | 1915 | 1.1 | 1923 | 11.5 |
|  |  |  |  | 1924 | 8.3[2] |

[1] As an index to the volume of unemployment in the years under consideration these trade-union percentages are the most reliable source of information available. For evidence of this the reader is referred to the detailed consideration of statistical sources given in Chapter IX.

[2] Mean of first three months.

Three points worthy of particular consideration for an estimation of the inevitability of unemployment insurance collapse are brought out by the chart. The first, that the mean percentage of unemployment during 1921 and 1922 was almost exactly twice as great as that of the previous depression period in 1908 and 1909, while even in 1923 the mean percentage of unemployment exactly equalled the evil record attained in 1879. It is, therefore, no more than just to call the unemployment of the post-war period unprecedented.

The second point to be observed is that the nine-year period 1912–20 (inclusive), during which the State system was supposed to be preparing for its time of test, contained four years in which unemployment was practically non-existent, while in the remaining five years it was well below the mean of the period 1875–1911. The third point is, that if 1904 is counted as a depression year — which it undoubtedly was — there had been at the end of 1920 a longer stretch in which to prepare for the seemingly inevitable cyclical depression than in any other period of good employment recorded. It is, therefore, no more than just to say that the post-war depression followed a period in which the absence of unemployment was, in modern times, unprecedented.

## MEAN UNEMPLOYMENT FROM 1912 TO 1923 NOT ABNORMAL

Care must be taken, moreover, not to attach undue importance to the height reached by the unemployment percentage in 1921–22. The problem is bi-dimensional — the horizontal measurements must be given adequate consideration if a just verdict is to be reached. To illustrate the importance of duration the chart also shows the mean percentage of employment during the two periods January, 1875, to December, 1911 (pre-insurance) and January, 1912, to December, 1922 (insurance). Mean unemployment over a pre-insurance period of thirty-seven years was

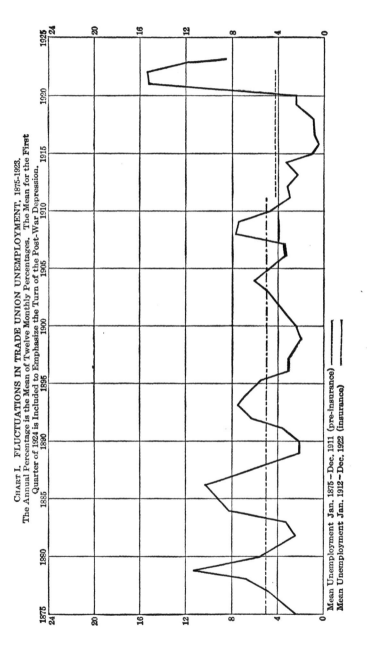

CHART I. FLUCTUATIONS IN TRADE UNION UNEMPLOYMENT, 1875-1923.
The Annual Percentage is the Mean of Twelve Monthly Percentages. The Mean for the First
Quarter of 1924 is Included to Emphasize the Turn of the Post-War Depression.

Mean Unemployment Jan. 1875 – Dec. 1911 (pre-insurance) ————
Mean Unemployment Jan. 1912 – Dec. 1922 (insurance) ————

exactly five per cent. In the insurance period up to January, 1923, when the State-operated system had ceased to be insurance in all but name, the mean unemployment was 4.28 per cent, or lower by more than seven tenths of one per cent than the mean unemployment for the first period. In other words, the national unemployment insurance system proved unable successfully to outride a cycle from the end of one depression to the turning-point of the next (as the chart shows plainly), during which the mean unemployment was less than that of the preceding thirty-seven years. Even if we are unfairly generous and take the mean unemployment of the insurance period up to January, 1924, the situation is not materially altered. The average for the second period is still less than that for the first: 4.88 per cent as against 5.00 per cent.

It may be said, then, that State-operated unemployment insurance was unable to stand a strain no heavier than should have been anticipated. But to have shown this is not at all the same thing as showing that the ineffectiveness during the post-war depression was inevitable. There is a very real danger that because of the record of degeneration of the Government system an indictment against the whole principle of unemployment insurance may be drawn. Such an indictment on the evidence which has been put forward would be a most grave injustice. This study has so far been concerned primarily with the facts of the collapse of the State-operated system. The main reasons for the undue rapidity of this collapse have been mentioned, but no attempt has hitherto been made to estimate their real importance.

The first reason why the Unemployment Fund was obliterated so quickly is found in the fact that the 1920 Act came into operation at the very end of a period of good employment and at the beginning of a period of depression. During the nine-year period of preparation contributions to the fund were for the first five years coming in only in respect of an average of approximately 2,250,000 insured work-people; and for the next four years only in respect of an average of approximately 4,000,000. During the period of depression, on the other hand, there were from the beginning 12,000,000 insured work-people with a potential right to unemployment insurance benefit.

The rapidity with which this drain exhausted the Unemployment Fund may be understood by examining Ministry of Labor statistics for the year 1921.[1] During this year the average weekly number of wholly unemployed workers drawing unemployment benefit or out-of-work donation was 1,487,000.

Individual payments to the number of about 88,000,000 were made during the year totaling (exclusive of £500,000 expended in O.W.D.) as follows:

| | |
|---|---|
| Unemployment benefit . . . . . . . | £57,500,000 |
| Unemployed    workers'    dependants' grants . . . . . . . . . . . . | 1,100,000 |
| | £58,600,000 |

The income of the Unemployment Fund and the Unemployed Workers' Dependants' Fund together during the year amounted to £31,600,000, made up as follows:

| | |
|---|---|
| Contributions of employers . . . . . | £11,750,000 |
| Contributions of work-people . . . . | 10,750,000 |
| State contribution . . . . . . . . | 6,500,000 |
| Contributions of Service Departments under Section 41 of 1920 Act . . . | 1,500,000 |
| Interest on Investments . . . . . . | 1,100,000 |
| | £31,600,000 |

In order to meet the cost of benefit and administrative expenditure, the entire accumulated balance of £22,700,000 in the Unemployment Fund had to be swept away as well as an Exchequer loan of £7,600,000, repayable with interest. And this for the single year of 1921.

### INSOLVENCY COULD HAVE BEEN POSTPONED

It is, of course, impossible to say with scientific accuracy what the balance of the Unemployment Fund would have

[1] *Labor Gazette*, April, 1922, pp. 156–57.

been at the beginning of the depression period if the situation then had been as favorable as possible — that is, if the full twelve million work-people insured in 1920 had been insured in 1912. A careful computation, however, indicates that the difference would have been sufficient to have retained the Fund in solvency throughout 1922 in spite of the wholesale removal of restrictions on benefit payments during the depression period.

Reference to the table on page 29 shows that the balance of contributions over benefit during the first year of national unemployment insurance amounted to £1,791,720.[1] As the trades at first insured were ones chosen partly because of their high normal percentage of unemployment, it is fair to estimate that, if twelve million instead of two and a quarter million work-people had then been insured, the gross balance for the year would have been at least five and one third times as great, or about £9,500,000. As the seven years July, 1913, to July, 1920, were, with a single exception, years in which employment was decidedly better than in the first insurance year, it is fair to estimate that with twelve million work-people insured throughout this period the Fund would in July, 1920, have shown a gross balance of quite eight times £9,500,000, or approximately £76,000,000. Deducting all refunds, administrative expenses charged on the Fund, and other items which could have reduced this gross total[2] there would, on the hypothesis taken, still have been a net balance of some £67,000,000 at the end of the eighth insurance year.

Such a balance would have been far more than ample to have maintained the Fund in solvency up to the end

---

[1] The benefits during the fiscal year (April–March) are here compared with the contributions during the insurance year (July–June). But the fact that the twelve-month periods compared do not quite synchronize makes very little difference and may be overlooked in this estimate of "what might have been."

[2] Making due allowance for the increased numbers supposed to have been insured, but not counting additional interest which would have accrued to the invested fund.

of the tenth insurance year, even with the increased benefits and relaxed restrictions which were allowed during the depression period. In January, 1921, when the Fund was at its maximum, it showed a net balance of £22,750,000. By July, 1922, this balance had been converted into a deficit of £15,400,000, giving a net drain of £38,150,000 in eighteen months. This drain, which as matters actually stood, was sufficient to reduce the Fund to an insolvency which could be met only by heavy borrowing from the Treasury, need not have rendered it insolvent at all. From the previous computation, it will be seen that there might have been a balance of approximately £29,000,000 still on hand in July, 1922. This would have been sufficient to pay the entire Out-of-Work Donation to civilians [1] and still have left £7,125,000 in the Fund after eighteen months of severe depression. Assuming the deficit to have mounted at an average rate of £2,000,000 a month, which is extreme, this surplus would have postponed the advent of insolvency to the end of 1922, without considering the beneficial effect of the Dependants' Grants regulations on the Fund.

The above reasoning is based on the assumption that it would have been administratively possible in 1912 to launch a full-blown scheme of national unemployment insurance covering practically the whole industrial population. But even if it is agreed that such action would not have been feasible, the argument that the post-war débâcle was inevitable does not hold. If (as was urged by many) in 1916 an Act with the scope of the Act of 1920 had been passed, sufficient reserves would still have been amassed to have carried a solvent fund through the months January, 1921, to July, 1922. In July, 1916, the Fund showed a net balance of £6,711,504. In the next four insurance years, with only about four million workers insured, the annual balance of contributions over benefit averaged more than £3,300,000.[2] Had three times as many workers been in-

[1] Cf. p. 32.
[2] Cf. Table I, p. 29, and first footnote on p. 75.

sured during these four years it is a fair estimate that
£39,500,000 gross — say £35,000,000 net — would have
been added to the reserve. As the actual balance in July,
1916, was more than six and one half million pounds the
indication is that under the circumstances postulated
there would have been a balance of at least £41,500,000
in July, 1920. Even this sum would have left a balance of
nearly four million pounds still on hand in July, 1922,
though it would not have sufficed to dispense with even the
civilian Out-of-Work Donation.

### The Device of Insurance is not Indicted

Therefore it does not necessarily follow from the post-
war collapse of the national insurance system that such an
outcome was inevitable. The facts do not of themselves
jeopardize the principle on which unemployment insurance
is based. Theoretically, at least, it is manifest that lack
of foresight and not extent of unemployment was the
fundamental cause of the collapse. The indictment, it
appears, should be drawn rather against the mechanical
and limited method of State administration than against
the institution of unemployment insurance as a device for
storing up the surplus purchasing power of good times
for use in the lean years of depression. Not the tool, but
the way it has been wielded, has made the work unsatisfactory.

The second main reason for the rapid collapse of the
Unemployment Fund is found in such steps as the introduction of "uncovenanted benefit," forced on the Government because of the inadequacy of its preparations for the
depression period. It would, of course, have been possible
to maintain the solvency of the Fund without large Treasury
loans, no matter how acute the depression, simply by refusing benefit to all except the small minority who could
have proved eligibility if the various restrictions had been
maintained or (in case of necessity) made even more
rigorous. Instead the Government hastened the deficit

by removing restrictions to such an extent [1] that a large part of unemployment insurance work became little better than a strictly regularized system of doles masquerading under the title of "uncovenanted benefit."

On the other hand, to have kept the Fund solvent by maintaining the pre-depression restrictions on benefit would have meant an amount of relief so pitiably small, and so soon exhausted, as speedily to have swept away the whole pretense that such a system of insurance can be an adequate "second line of defence" during a depression period. Because in Great Britain State-operated unemployment insurance had been accepted as the major defence against unemployment, and all other measures, including the efficiency of the Employment Exchanges, subordinated to the development of this form of unemployment insurance, it was only natural that in the time of test, unemployment insurance machinery should have been twisted and distorted in the effort to make it a fairly adequate vehicle of relief.

The only outcome which could have justified such sacrifice of principle would have been success in focussing the relief of unemployment as a responsibility of the National Government. If the Ministry of Labor was to sacrifice unemployment insurance in order to give relief it should at least have given relief sufficient to have relieved local government of that burden. But the compromise attempted in Great Britain failed ignobly. Although the system of unemployment insurance practically ceased to function as insurance, it was not able to provide adequate relief. Not for a century has there been anything which even approximates the burden of relief which fell on local authorities during the very months in which unemployment insurance was itself going insolvent in trying to handle the problem. Because of its obvious bearing on an analysis

[1] Admittedly, it was the fear of nation-wide rioting, if not more serious social disorders, that actuated the panic legislation by which the unemployment insurance program was destroyed.

of the effectiveness of unemployment insurance, some attention to the spread of recourse to Poor Law relief will be given here.

## THE SYSTEM OF DUAL RELIEF

Fifty years of effort, it has been pointed out,[1] was spent by the pioneers of unemployment relief in Great Britain in trying to separate the treatment of unemployment from the undiscriminating outdoor relief given to able-bodied paupers under the Poor Law. Unemployment insurance, it was hoped, would assist this separation, but obviously the inadequacy of the scale of benefits decided upon would make it impossible to prevent insured workers from still having recourse to Poor Law relief in times of distress. Those who drew up the 1911 Act therefore adopted a compromise. While receipt of benefit was not to exclude any unemployed person from Poor Law relief, the guardians, as custodians of the rate-payers' money, were not to ignore the fact that the Government was now using national taxation for unemployment relief. The part of the 1911 Act (Section 109) which sanctioned this dual system of relief read as follows: "In granting outdoor relief to a person in receipt of or entitled to receive any benefit under this Act, a Board of Guardians shall not take into consideration any such benefit except so far as such benefit exceeds five shillings a week." The 1920 Act (Section 27) followed an identical policy, local relieving authorities being told not to take unemployment benefit into account "except in so far as it exceeds ten shillings a week."

A system under which two different sets of authorities are made separately responsible for financial relief in case of unemployment is clearly one which invites fraud. While the system of double relief to the unemployed — unemployment insurance benefit from the State, and relief in money and kind from the local Boards of Guardians — led

[1] In Chapter I.

to no scandal so long as employment was good and the safeguards on payment of benefit were rigidly maintained, trouble naturally arose as soon as these safeguards were loosened. During the depression period there have, for instance, been numerous "delayed claims" to benefit — claims where an appeal has been lodged or where some further investigation has been deemed advisable — in which arrears of benefit have subsequently been paid. Admittedly this has resulted in many cases of what is called by employment officials "leakage," where an unemployed person has received for the same period both the full scale of relief from the Guardians and full unemployment benefit from the State. Often the result has been that for short periods more money has been handed out to an unemployed worker than he could have made by working at his trade.

Under the Unemployment Insurance Act of April, 1922 (Section 14), it was laid down that "the authority having power to grant the [outdoor] relief shall take into account the amount of the Benefit," [1] a change of phraseology calculated to put responsibility more directly on the Boards of Guardians, and an elaborate system of coöperation designed to check most of this "leakage" was in May, 1922, worked out between local Poor Law authorities and local Employment Exchanges. But these safeguards were at best only able to check dishonest utilization of the system of double relief. The main problem, which has been the tremendous extent to which double relief has increased in spite of the loosening of unemployment insurance restrictions, remained untouched. Unfortunately, it is impossible to obtain precise information of the extent to which dual relief was utilized during the depression period. An analysis made at Birmingham shows that of persons there

---

[1] In other words, the whole of the benefit and not only so much of it as exceeded a certain sum was to be considered. This change was first inaugurated by the Unemployed Workers' Dependants Act of November, 1921. It temporarily checked the recourse to Poor Law relief (Cf. Table VI, p. 83).

receiving unemployment benefit at January 17, 1923, about 17.3 per cent were also drawing Poor Law relief.[1]

## THE RUSH TO THE POOR LAW

Table VI and the accompanying chart[2] show, for thirty-one of the principal urban areas of Great Britain, the monthly alteration since October, 1919, (a) in the number of persons given outdoor relief, (b) in the number of persons given indoor relief, (c) in the rate per 10,000 of estimated population receiving relief of one or other of these two sorts. The chief points brought out by these statistics of Poor Law relief, covering districts with about 18,000,000 inhabitants and including by far the greater part of the industrial population of Great Britain, are:

That the numbers in receipt of indoor relief — almost altogether non-able-bodied — have, relatively speaking, remained almost stationary.

That the numbers in receipt of outdoor relief — the able-bodied unemployed and their dependents — increased by over six hundred per cent in the eighteen months after the Unemployment Insurance Act of 1920 went into effect.

That the various Acts whereby unemployment insurance restrictions were removed exercised a very slight check on

[1] *Report on National Unemployment Insurance to July, 1923*, p. 15. A picture of the results of dual relief, in an extreme case, is given in the Government White Paper, *Report of Special Inquiry, under Direction of Ministry of Health, into Expenditure of Poplar Board of Guardians, 1922*. A reply by George Lansbury in the *Labor Monthly* for June, 1922, stoutly defending from the social viewpoint the additional expenditure of the Poplar (Labor Party) Guardians on unemployment relief, should also be referred to. At this time the scale of local unemployment relief in the London Borough of Poplar was 12s. 6d. a week plus rent for a single adult, 20s. plus rent for man and wife, 26s. 6d. for man and wife with one child, and 5s. additional for each additional child. The whole of unemployment insurance benefit, the whole of parents' earnings, and a part of every child's earnings when over 15s. a week, were deductible from this scale. The scale of local relief in this London Borough was much above the average.

[2] Compiled from statistics published monthly by the *Labor Gazette*, from data supplied by the Ministry of Health in England and the Board of Health in Scotland.

## 82 UNEMPLOYMENT RELIEF IN GREAT BRITAIN

the recourse to Poor Law relief. The effect of the Act of March, 1921, for instance, is imperceptible, due to the neutralizing effect of the stoppage of work in the coal industry.

That the cumulative effect of unemployment has been largely met by recourse to the Poor Law. The steady improvement in employment during the first four months of 1923, for instance, made very little difference in the number obtaining this form of relief.[1]

That, in industrial areas at least, unemployment relief has, in spite of the State program, become far and away the most important burden on the Poor Law.[2]

That whenever "gap periods" in uncovenanted benefit have been enforced the numbers seeking Poor Law relief have increased.

TABLE VI. POOR LAW RELIEF IN 31 INDUSTRIAL AREAS OF GREAT BRITAIN

| DATE | NUMBER OF PERSONS IN RECEIPT OF POOR LAW RELIEF ON ONE DAY IN SPECIFIED MONTH | | | RATE OF TOTAL PER 10,000 OF ESTIMATED POPULATION |
|---|---|---|---|---|
| | Indoor | Outdoor | Total | |
| 1920 | | | | |
| Jan. | 107,058 | 123,380 | 230,438 | 130 |
| Feb. | 107,945 | 124,668 | 232,613 | 131 |
| Mar. | 108,380 | 126,363 | 234,743 | 132 |
| Apr. | 107,806 | 126,809 | 234,615 | 132 |
| May | 106,351 | 128,316 | 234,667 | 132 |
| June | 105,541 | 129,169 | 234,710 | 132 |
| July | 105,452 | 131,775 | 237,227 | 134 |
| Aug. | 105,496 | 132,594 | 238,090 | 134 |
| Sept. | 106,336 | 134,404 | 240,740 | 136 |
| Oct. | 108,751 | 144,761 | 253,512 | 143 |
| Nov. | 111,275 | 160,407 | 271,682 | 153 |
| Dec. | 112,964 | 177,994 | 290,958 | 164 |
| 1921 | | | | |
| Jan. | 115,694 | 202,717 | 318,411 | 179 |
| Feb. | 116,960 | 214,042 | 331,002 | 186 |

[1] Cf. Table XIII, p. 135.

[2] This is a complete reversal of the pre-war situation, where the able-bodied unemployed formed only a small proportion of those receiving Poor Law relief. (See Majority and Minority *Reports of the Royal Commission on the Poor Laws*.)

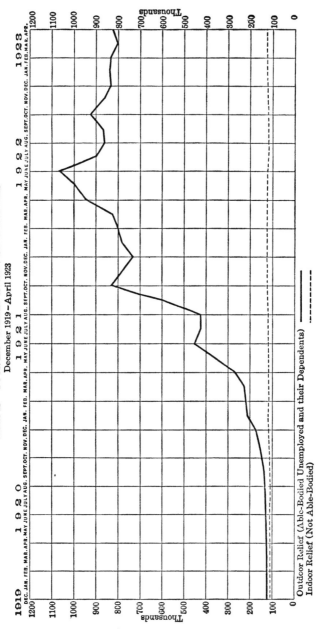

CHART II    POOR LAW RELIEF IN INDUSTRIAL AREAS
December 1919 – April 1923

Outdoor Relief (Able-Bodied Unemployed and their Dependents) ——————
Indoor Relief (Not Able-Bodied) - - - - - - - -

TABLE VI — (*Continued*).   POOR LAW RELIEF

| DATE | NUMBER OF PERSONS IN RECEIPT OF POOR LAW RELIEF ON ONE DAY IN SPECIFIED MONTH | | | RATE OF TOTAL PER 10,000 OF ESTIMATED POPULATION |
|---|---|---|---|---|
| | Indoor | Outdoor | Total | |
| **1921** | | | | |
| Mar. | 116,428 | 224,488 | 340,916 | 191 |
| Apr. | 116,703 | 275,732 | 392,435 | 220 |
| May | 116,661 | 362,404 | 479,065 | 269 |
| June | 115,692 | 455,359 | 571,051 | 320 |
| July | 115,955 | 427,278 | 543,233 | 305a |
| Aug. | 116,946 | 428,463 | 545,409 | 306 |
| Sept. | 119,823 | 599,073 | 718,896 | 403 |
| Oct. | 121,436 | 831,085 | 952,521 | 549 |
| Nov. | 122,647 | 783,971 | 906,618 | 522b |
| Dec. | 124,838 | 732,156 | 856,994 | 494 |
| **1922** | | | | |
| Jan. | 127,104 | 791,635 | 918,739 | 529 |
| Feb. | 126,810 | 800,498 | 927,308 | 534 |
| Mar. | 124,803 | 828,302 | 953,105 | 549 |
| Apr. | 123,379 | 946,321 | 1,069,700 | 616 |
| May | 121,717 | 991,156 | 1,112,873 | 641 |
| June | 120,603 | 1,064,824 | 1,185,427 | 683 |
| July | 120,311 | 901,192 | 1,021,503 | 588c |
| Aug. | 119,981 | 861,162 | 981,143 | 565 |
| Sept. | 120,717 | 876,020 | 996,737 | 574 |
| Oct. | 122,487 | 926,417 | 1,048,904 | 604 |
| Nov. | 124,473 | 867,629 | 992,102 | 572 |
| Dec. | 125,231 | 836,839 | 962,070 | 554 |
| **1923** | | | | |
| Jan. | 126,454 | 846,019 | 972,473 | 560 |
| Feb. | 127,536 | 832,660 | 960,196 | 553 |
| Mar. | 126,315 | 798,276 | 924,591 | 533 |
| Apr. | 125,271 | 832,572 | 957,843 | 552d |
| May | 123,321 | 772,713 | 896,034 | 516 |
| June | 121,986 | 767,415 | 889,401 | 512 |
| July | 121,406 | 825,741 | 947,147 | 546 |
| Aug. | 121,143 | 779,225 | 900,368 | 519 |
| Sept. | 121,602 | 783,875 | 905,477 | 522 |
| Oct. | 123,460 | 792,732 | 916,192 | 528 |
| Nov. | 125,085 | 743,698 | 868,783 | 491 |
| Dec. | 126,286 | 721,998 | 848,284 | 479 |
| **1924** | | | | |
| Jan. | 129,095 | 779,799 | 908,894 | 514 |
| Feb. | 129,781 | 771,342 | 901,123 | 509 |
| Mar. | 127,621 | 700,313 | 827,934 | 468e |
| Apr. | 124,703 | 687,355 | 812,058 | 459 |
| May | 122,030 | 656,409 | 778,439 | 440 |

a Unemployment Insurance Act of July, 1921.
b Unemployed Workers' Dependants Act (see footnote to page 80).
c "Gap" in benefit cut from five weeks to one week by Unemployment Insurance Act of July, 1922 (see page 64).
d Two-week "gap" in Fourth Special Period operative for those who had been drawing continuous benefit since November, 1922.
e "Gap" in benefit abolished from February 21, 1924.

The table below illustrates the degree to which unemployment insurance benefit was being extended during the same period that the rush to the Poor Law set in. A single locality (Liverpool) where unemployment has been very severe without being at all exceptional, has been chosen for this purpose.[1]

TABLE VII. NUMBERS RECEIVING NATIONAL UNEMPLOYMENT RELIEF AND LOCAL OUTDOOR POOR RELIEF IN LIVERPOOL

| DATE | NATIONAL UNEMPLOYMENT RELIEF (in Liverpool City) | | | LOCAL OUTDOOR POOR RELIEF (in Liverpool District) |
|---|---|---|---|---|
| | U. I. | O.W.D. | Total | |
| 1920 | | | | |
| Jan. | 1,316 | 24,168 | 25,484 | 8,898 |
| Feb. | 1,037 | 17,511 | 18,548 | 9,015 |
| Mar. | 1,106 | 18,290 | 19,396 | 9,123 |
| 1921 | | | | |
| Jan. | 18,322 | 26,675 | 44,997 | 11,632 |
| Feb. | 27,133 | 29,020 | 56,153 | 12,206 |
| Mar. | 36,341 | 25,640 | 61,981 | 12,809 |
| 1922 | | | | |
| Jan. | 122,257 | 0 | 122,257 | 70,186 |
| Feb. | 128,275 | 0 | 128,275 | 72,719 |
| Mar. | 114,136 | 1 | 114,137 | 75,601 |

CHARGES THE STATE-OPERATED SYSTEM MUST FACE

The main points of evidence brought out in this chapter may now be recapitulated.

[1] A chief reason for the selection of Liverpool for the purpose of this table is the conservative nature of its local government. It was desirable to obtain an instance where charges of unnecessary outdoor relief, such as have been brought against certain Socialist Boards of Guardians (notably that for the district of Poplar, in London), could not for a moment be entertained.

Regarding the comparative degree of necessity in the Liverpool District, it may be noted that in March, 1922, this district ranked eighth highest in percentage of population receiving outdoor poor relief, out of the thirty-one principal industrial districts for which Poor Law relief statistics are published monthly in the Ministry of Labor Gazette.

The amounts paid out in Liverpool in National Unemployment Relief during these periods were:

| | U. I. | O.W.D. | Total |
|---|---|---|---|
| 1st Quarter 1920 | £2,031. 0.10 | £80,934. 4.2 | £82,985.5.0 |
| 1st Quarter 1921 | £50,496. 0. 4 | £74,871. 0.4 | £125,367.0.8 |
| 1st Quarter 1922 | £282,018.10.10 | £0.16.8 | £282,019.7.6 |

By the end of 1920, as a glance at the chart facing page 72 will indicate, a cyclical trade depression with its consequent unemployment was overdue. Steadily the opinion is gaining ground that this post-war depression was at bottom and in essentials a normal cyclical depression.[1] That the depression was exaggerated and complicated by the effects of the war and its aftermath goes without saying. This does not alter the fact that at the end of 1920 more than a decade had passed since the previous period of depression in Great Britain, and that this phenomenon, judging by its periodicity during a hundred years, was to have been expected.[2] Severe unemployment no later than the time at which it actually set in was a test which the State-controlled unemployment insurance system would almost certainly have had to face even without the war.

Nor was unemployment during that part of the depression up to January, 1923, by which time the principle of unemployment insurance had been largely discarded for the principle of continuous benefit, sufficiently acute to outweigh the years of exceptionally good employment which preceded. As has been shown mean unemployment was higher during the period, January, 1875, to December, 1911, than during the period, January, 1912, to December, 1922.

During the seventeen months from the end of January, 1921, to the beginning of July, 1922, the national unemployment insurance system not only absorbed all the financial reserves accumulated in eight good years, but plunged into a deficit which no insurance business conducted on business principles could have survived. For this collapse there were two main reasons: The first, that during the period of preparation contributions were only

[1] See, for instance, the introductory chapter to Lavington: *The Trade Cycle*. Also, *Business Cycles and Unemployment* (U.S. Dept. of Commerce, 1923), p. 1.

[2] "During the past century the interval from one depression to the next has varied from seven to eleven years." (Beveridge: *Unemployment*, p. 57.) The last previous depression in Great Britain was that of 1908-09.

coming in at the outset in respect of some 2,250,000 insured workers, and after 1916 in respect of about 4,000,000 insured workers, while from the very beginning of the depression period there were 12,000,000 insured workers with a potential right to benefit. The second main reason for collapse was the decision to break down the limitations on the receipt of benefit, allowing insurance progressively to approximate to a system of "uncovenanted" doles.

Although these considerations make it unfair to assert that the degeneration of the State-controlled unemployment insurance system was inevitable, they provide no basis for evading certain serious indictments:

(1) That under its first and (all things considered) not unduly rigorous test the British system ceased to be self-supporting with a rapidity which at least indicates that its efficacy was limited to times of good employment.

(2) That in spite of the sacrifice of principle whereby unemployment insurance degenerated to something very closely akin to the provision of doles, the State-operated system did not prevent a recourse to local relief through the Poor Law unprecedented in modern times. This failure on the part of the unemployment insurance system is the more marked because of the protracted and very expensive assistance afforded it by out-of-work donations.

(3) That at the very time when the increasing burden of relieving the unemployed was becoming intolerable for the local authorities, the national system of unemployment insurance was being twisted into an amorphous and incredibly complicated arrangement which at bottom closely resembled a centralized system of outdoor relief. In spite of this, by the middle of 1922 what amounted to local unemployment relief was being given under the Poor Law to seven out of every hundred people in thirty-one of the most important urban areas of Great Britain. Instead of supplanting this local relief unemployment insurance merely supplemented it.

A fourth major indictment of State-operated unemployment insurance remains for examination. It is that the system in its decline, even more than in its normal operation, has slowed down and choked the whole machinery of the Employment Exchanges in their primary function of organizing "the labor market."

# CHAPTER VII

## THE JUSTIFICATION OF THE BRITISH SYSTEM

BEFORE discussing the effect of unemployment insurance work on the basic objective of the Employment Exchanges (which is the coördination of unemployed workers with vacant jobs), it would seem advisable to utilize material already presented in an attempt to answer a question of fundamental importance — Has the British unemployment insurance system justified itself on economic grounds?

The success with which this question is dodged in the considerable body of literature devoted to unemployment relief is surprising. It would seem to be one of the first issues with which students of the subject would go to the mat. Yet contemporary studies of State-operated unemployment insurance are generally much more concerned with revisions by which the existing method might be improved than they are with any consideration of whether the existing method is sound at heart. One can only conclude that in the twelve years during which the system has been in operation it has become so familiar that the idea of questioning the principles on which it rests does not arise. Nevertheless, that question is one which the experience of the depression period brings sharply forward.

### ECONOMIC JUSTIFICATION OF STATE-OPERATED UNEMPLOYMENT INSURANCE

To justify itself on economic grounds it would seem that a system of State-operated unemployment insurance, the purpose of which is not to be confused with the different social function filled by Employment Exchanges, must accomplish one or more of four ends. It must either (1) diminish unemployment; or (2) render consumption more steady than income; or (3) centralize all responsibility for unemployment relief in a single organization, eliminating the confusion, fraud, and overlapping effort inevitable when several agencies share responsibility for the relief of the same unemployed work-people; or it must (4) provide relief at less expense to the taxpayer than could be given by the much simpler device of regulated doles.

It is, obviously, an insufficient defense of the present insurance system to say that it tends to distribute the economic losses of unemployment, and the expense of unemployment relief, over the entire community. Any regularized system of State doles, the necessary funds for which were obtained by equitable taxation, would have that effect, and probably in a way more just than that afforded by the State insurance system. For in levying flat contributory rates on employers and employees State-operated unemployment insurance makes no such delicate distinctions in incidence as does a carefully planned system of taxation. Manifestly, from the viewpoint of equitable distribution of burden, an insurance device is far from perfect which takes the same deduction from the pay envelope of the worker earning thirty shillings a week, and from the worker earning six pounds a week. The same applies to employers, some wealthy and others barely making ends meet, who pay identical contributions so long as they employ an identical number of adult insured workers of the same sex.

## DIMINUTION OF UNEMPLOYMENT

As regards the specific objectives of State-operated unemployment insurance outlined above, it is impossible to assert that the first, diminution of unemployment, has been attained to any perceptible extent. Theorists may argue that the British system has introduced factors tending to diminish unemployment. Hard experience indicates that this part of insurance theory does not work

out in practice.[1] Not only is it by no means always within
the power of the average manufacturing employer to control the rate of production, a power which goes back of
him to the wholesale merchant and banker. In addition
the possibility of giving the average employer a sufficient
financial incentive to reduce unemployment through the
penalizing effect of unemployment insurance, is very
questionable. Sir William Beveridge has shown for the
British system of unemployment insurance [2] that even if
benefits were raised to half of normal wages and the average
percentage of unemployment halved, the saving in contributions for the average employer would be less than
one half of one per cent of his wages bill. And he rightly
concludes that this would not suffice to make most employers take any pains to regularize employment in their
establishments.

### STEADYING OF CONSUMPTION

What has been the practical success of State-operated
unemployment insurance in achieving the second objective — steadying of individual consumption? Although
the question cannot be answered scientifically, there is
at hand sufficient evidence to give a considered opinion.

During the depression period it was the general taxation
program of the Government rather than the device of insurance which provided any steadying of consumption that
may have been achieved. Add to the sums borrowed from
the Treasury for unemployment insurance the direct Government contributions to the Unemployment Fund,[3] as well
as the large sums gathered by local taxation for local poor

[1] See pp. 38 and 125 for evidence that most of the petty, yet
complicated, devices for encouraging regularity of employment have
proved much more troublesome than effective in operation.

[2] In the *Manchester Guardian Commercial* of February 21, 1923,
p. 201.

[3] Under the Unemployment Insurance Acts of 1922 the State contribution to the Unemployment Fund amounted to something over one
third of the employers' and employed persons' contributions combined.
From the Armistice to March 1, 1924, the State paid £38,063,000;

relief, amounting to approximately £74,350,000 for the two fiscal years 1921–23. Considering the magnitude of these charges on the taxpayer, one perceives clearly that the insurance payments made by employers and employees have been only a part, indeed well under half, of the sums expended in unemployment relief, without taking the cost of relief works into consideration at all. And since a serious falling-off in consumption was seemingly little ameliorated by unemployment insurance plus State grants of one form or another, it is obvious that the effect, if self-supporting insurance alone had been relied on, would have been even less noticeable. If consumers' demands within Great Britain were sufficient to absorb the production of which that nation is now normally capable, the artificial maintenance of wage-earners' incomes might improve employment perceptibly.[1] But more forceful than this theory is the fact that when the foreign trade of a country like Great Britain suffers marked decline, loss of national income becomes a factor much more pronounced in its effects than unequal distribution of national income.

The belief that the indirect regularization of workers' expenditure obtained through compulsory insurance would tend to steady production over the trade cycle, was a factor in the establishment of State-operated unemployment insurance in Great Britain. With higher scales of contributions and benefits in force from the beginning, it is quite possible that results in this direction would have been attained. But developments of the depression period show that the idea has been less valid in practice than in theory. It has been pointed out that the so-called Insurance Industry, in setting up a Special Scheme of its own under the Act of 1920, eliminated employees' contributions from

employers, £54,311,000; and employed persons, £49,463,000 in contributions under the various Unemployment Insurance Acts.

[1] An interesting presentation of the thesis that much might be done to eliminate cyclical depressions by a more equitable distribution of the national income is given by J. A. Hobson in *The Economics of Unemployment*.

its program.[1] Dropping the work-people's contributions is also a characteristic of the proposals for revising unemployment insurance procedure made by Sir William Beveridge in the *Manchester Guardian Commercial* article referred to on page 90. These incidents are serious evidence that State-operated unemployment insurance has actually accomplished little in steadying consumption.

"There is *prima facie* ground," wrote Professor A. C. Pigou in 1913, "for holding that the evil consequences of unemployment might be reduced by legal enactments designed to induce workpeople to invest a larger proportion of their resources than they naturally tend to do in the work of rendering their consumption more steady."[2] When a decade later, an authority like Sir William Beveridge is found supporting the movement to dispense with workers' contributions altogether, the indication is strong that results have not justified the effort expended on this theory.

CENTRALIZATION OF RESPONSIBILITY

In considering the success of State-operated unemployment insurance in attaining the third objective — centralization of responsibility for unemployment relief — it seems unnecessary to add anything to the analysis given in the preceding chapter of recourse to the Poor Law during the depression period. Throughout 1921, 1922, and 1923 the national insurance system by itself proved quite incapable of meeting the responsibility for unemployment relief. Nor was the enormous increase in outdoor relief under the Poor Law the only way in which the insufficiency of unemployment insurance was demonstrated. Meals for school children provided by local education authorities, although a minor item in the total expenditure on unemployment relief, became a considerable factor during the depression period. Just over one seventh of the school population of the country were provided with an

[1] See p. 49, footnote.
[2] *Unemployment*, p. 221.

average of one hundred meals each in this manner during the fiscal year ending March 31, 1922.[1] And on April 4, 1922, it was announced in Parliament that advances by the Board of Education for this purpose would be limited to £300,000 during the fiscal year 1922–23, the Government having decided "that it is impossible to acquiesce in a continuance of the present arrangement, under which, in abnormal periods, a considerable part of the burden of poor relief may be thrown upon the education rate and the Vote of the Board of Education."

Turn now to the fourth of the questions which this chapter attempts to answer. That the State-operated unemployment insurance system came to approximate a system of strictly regulated doles during the depression period has been shown. In the process was it saved by the contributions of employers and employed from being as costly to the State as direct monetary relief? At first thought the answer would appear to be an unquestionable affirmative. Nevertheless, analysis gives results which modify that view surprisingly.

RELATIVE EXPENSE OF INSURANCE AND DOLES

It is possible, by taking the maximum weekly benefit payable under each of the Unemployment Insurance Acts and multiplying this sum by the number of weeks for which benefit was allowed under each Act, to obtain the maximum benefit payable in the course of a year at every period of the unemployment insurance program. Similarly, the proceed to the Unemployment Fund, exclusive of the State contribution, can be calculated by multiplying the number of weeks in which benefit was not payable by the weekly contributions of employer and employed person added together. In the comparison which is to be made, this method, obviously, gives un-

[1] *The Third Winter of Unemployment*, p. 49. "In a school population of 4,110,000, children numbering 592,000 received 60,676,000 meals in the year ending March 31, 1922."

employment insurance the benefit of the doubt. For it assumes that the unemployed worker drawing full benefit was in whole-time employment and paying contributions during that part of the year in which he was ineligible for benefit.

Subtracting the maximum proceed to the Fund from the maximum benefit payable out of the Fund there is obtained the per capita annual deficit in respect of an unemployed worker drawing the full benefit allowed. For the period of benefit allowed under each Act this deficit is the sum which might have been paid to the unemployed worker as an outright dole, instead of as insurance, without additional cost to the State. The comparison, it may be worth noting, is not at all invalidated by the fact that many insured workers failed to draw the full benefit permissible under the various Acts. Those who were able to dispense with unemployment insurance benefit would also have dispensed with doles. Nor is it invalidated by the fact that a large part of the money paid out in benefits by the State was received not from general taxation but from a special levy on productive industry — the compulsory unemployment insurance contributions from employers and employed workers. In effect these contributions amount to no more than a special tax on industry for the specific purpose of unemployment relief. With an outright dole program, this tax might have been levied more equitably. The obvious blunder of making employers pay higher for giving employment during the depression period could at least have been concealed.

The results of this analysis, in the case of an adult male wage earner ineligible for receipt of Dependants' Grants,[1] are given in Table VIII, on the opposite page. This table clearly shows that from the outset State-operated

[1] By causing an increase in the contributions in respect of all insured workers, grants to the dependants of the unemployed have proved extremely helpful to the Unemployment Fund (cf. p. 59). The practice, of course, is in itself a vitiation of the principles of real insurance.

TABLE VIII. THE RELATIVE EXPENSE OF UNEMPLOYMENT INSURANCE AND DOLES

In the case of an Adult Male Worker drawing Maximum Benefit, but ineligible for Dependants' Grants

| ACT | BENEFIT PERIOD (per Annum) | AMOUNT OF WEEKLY BENEFIT (£ s. d.) | MAXIMUM BENEFIT PAYABLE IN YEAR (£ s. d.) | MAXIMUM PROCEED (Exclusive of State Contribution) FOR REMAINDER OF YEAR (£ s. d.) | POTENTIAL DEFICIT (£ s. d.) | WEEKLY DOLE PAYABLE WITHOUT EXTRA COST TO STATE (£ s. d.) | PERCENTAGE OF BENEFIT PAYABLE AS DOLE WITHOUT EXTRA COST FOR ENTIRE BENEFIT PERIOD |
|---|---|---|---|---|---|---|---|
| 1911 | 15 Weeks | — 7 — | 5 5 — | — 15 5 | 4 9 7 | — 5 11.67 | 85.3 |
| 1914 | 15 " | — 7 — | 5 5 — | — 15 5 | 4 9 7 | — 5 11.67 | 85.3 |
| 1916 | 15 " | — 7 — | 5 5 — | — 15 5 | 4 9 7 | — 5 11.67 | 85.3 |
| 1919 | 15 " | — 11 — | 8 15 — | — 15 5 | 7 19 7 | — 10 7.67 | 96.7 |
| 1920 | 15 " | — 15 — | 11 5 — | 1 4 8 | 10 0 4 | — 13 4.27 | 89.0 |
| 1921 (March) | 24 " | 1 — — | 24 — — | 1 5 8 | 22 14 4 | — 18 11.17 | 94.7 |
| 1921 (July) | 33 " | — 15 — | 24 15 — | 1 3 9 | 23 11 3 | — 14 3 | 95.0 |
| 1922 (April) | 29.8 " | — 15 — | 22 7 — | 1 15 1.8 | 20 11 10.2 | — 13 10 | 92.2 |
| 1922 (July) | 35.75 " | — 15 — | 26 16 3 | 1 5 8.75 | 25 10 6.25 | — 14 8.32 | 95.2 |
| 1923 (March) | 46 " | — 15 — | 34 10 — | — 9 6 | 34 0 6 | — 14 9.52 | 98.6 |

unemployment insurance has had from the financial standpoint little advantage over a system of outright relief in which dole periods would have been limited as were benefit periods in the Acts as they stand. Moreover, Table VIII does not take administrative expenses into account. The large proportion of revenue which these have swallowed may be appreciated by referring to Table I on page 29. In the financial years 1912–13 and again in 1920–21 (years in which the original and the extended Acts were launched), the ratio of administrative expenses amounted to about 23 per cent of total revenue. In 1922–23 it fell as low as 10.3 per cent and for 1923–24 it was estimated in advance at 8.3 per cent, this sharp reduction being partly due to the increase in rates of contributions. The huge sums which have gone into the complex administration of State-operated unemployment insurance have probably made the system actually more costly than would have been an outright system of doles equal in amount and payable for the same periods as the insurance benefit. For these outright doles would have necessitated much less additional expenditure to that required for the ordinary placing work of the Employment Exchanges. There is no doubt that they would have been a cheaper method of relief in so far as those drawing full "uncovenanted benefit" were concerned.[1]

---

[1] A curious inconsistency in official information from the Ministry of Labor may be noted at this point. In June, 1920, Mr. T. W. Phillips, Principal Assistant Secretary of the Ministry of Labor, quoted an estimate of £644,000 as the cost of administering unemployment insurance as a separate factor in the financial year 1919–20 (Cmd. 1140 of 1921, p. 21). He added (*loc. cit.*): "Of course that sort of allocation" (between the administrative expenses of unemployment insurance and the administrative expenses of ordinary Employment Exchange work) "must be an estimate; the whole of the work is done by the same staff as a rule, and in the same office." Yet the recently published *Report on National Unemployment Insurance to July, 1923,* carrying the signature of the same Mr. Phillips, gives (p. 157) figures down to odd pounds of the cost of administration of unemployment insurance, with a sum total (£558,262) for the financial year 1919–20 over thirteen per cent less than the estimate made three years earlier.

The direction of this discrepancy is the more perplexing since Mr. Phillips says in the *Report to July, 1923* (p. 13) that "the administrative expenses of the Unemployment Insurance Scheme . . . cover not merely the organization required for collecting contributions and assessing and paying benefit, but also the whole cost of the Employment Exchanges so far as they deal with insured persons." Reference to Cmd. 1140 of 1921, p. 21, shows that the interpretation of "administrative expenses" was less inclusive when their total was put thirteen per cent higher, which is decidedly illogical, to say the least. However, I use these figures from the Report of 1923 (noting this peculiarity) in the last column of Table I on page 29 of this book. They are the only source of information available as to the cost of administration of State-operated unemployment insurance since its inception.

# CHAPTER VIII

## THE WORK OF THE EMPLOYMENT EXCHANGES

CONSIDERATION of the effect of unemployment insurance on the Employment Exchanges in their function as labor-placing agencies may usefully be prefaced by a brief description of a typical Exchange, a summary of routine work, and consideration of the major difficulties encountered in the daily course. For without some knowledge of the nature of the Exchanges and the procedure of employment work, it is impossible to give any clear idea of the extent to which unemployment insurance has complicated and hampered fulfillment of their primary duty of placing work-people in employment.

Out of a large number of Employment Exchanges in different parts of England, the work of which the author has been privileged to inspect, the Stepney Exchange, located on the edge of the East End of London, may be chosen as representative. Covering the Whitechapel area this Exchange caters to a large un-English population. But as the Government has done little to differentiate between native and alien in its unemployment policy this circumstance is immaterial.[1] What makes the Stepney Exchange particularly interesting is that it dates back to the period of the Unemployed Workmen Act of 1905 and has a long record of efficient service well maintained during the depression period, which made it one of the busiest of London Exchanges. Except in the matter of premises, many of which are worse and a few somewhat

[1] The most important discrimination is found in the rule that an alien who has resided in Great Britain for less than six months must not be submitted for any vacancy if suitable British workmen are available. Cf. Cmd. 1140 of 1921, p. 50, par. 32 (2).

better than those at Stepney, the description of the operation of this Exchange during 1922 would be equally applicable to any in Great Britain.

At this time the Stepney Exchange was located in a large three-story building, originally a clothing warehouse, and (like most Exchange premises) only rented by the Government. Very little outlay on equipment had been allowed, and most of the offices, such as that of the pay clerk and that used by the Local Employment Committee, were merely screened off in what had been large storage rooms. The building was divided into two main sections with separate entrances for men and for women. The juvenile division was in another building close by, as with most Exchanges. Except for separating skilled and unskilled workers, and separate provision for the handling of dockers and seamen, there was no further attempt to differentiate applicants, this being accomplished in the registration.

Use of the Exchange is not rigidly restricted either to those who inhabit the district or to those who have had their employment therein, but the fact that the country is so well covered with Exchanges automatically achieves this result. In July, 1923, there were 385 Employment Exchanges in operation in Great Britain. In addition there were then 780 Branch Employment Offices — small agencies in less important centers, generally manned by part-time officials.

### Routine Work of the Exchanges

The applicant, falling out of work, calls at the Exchange and enters his claim for unemployment benefit. If in an insured trade his Unemployment Book is "lodged" and he is given a form (U. I. A. 40) as receipt. The applicant gives the necessary assurance that, although out of work, willing to work, and capable of work, he is unable to obtain employment. He is registered according to an occupational classification,[1] and details of his industrial experience are taken.

The first step after taking the claim is to refer to the applicant's previous employer, asking the reason for his leaving employment. Upon receipt of any information which would invalidate the claim to benefit, the matter is referred for decision to the insurance officer who is attached to every Exchange. The applicant has the right of appeal to the Court of Referees against an unfavorable decision by an insurance officer, and is always informed of this privilege. From this tribunal, composed of one or more members chosen to represent employers, with an equal number of members chosen to represent insured contributors, and a chairman appointed by the Minister of Labor, further appeal may under certain circumstances be made to the umpire, a Crown official. The decision of the umpire is final.[2] Some idea of the complexity of cases arising under the Unemployment Insurance Acts may be gathered from the fact that 8361 separate cases were submitted to the umpire for final decision between the coming into operation of the Act of 1920 (November 8, 1920) and July 1, 1923. Of these 2269 were allowed and 6092 disallowed. A sample case, illustrating the care with which decisions are made by the umpire, is given in Appendix III.

If the report from the employer is favorable to the claimant, or if (as frequently happens) no reply is received, the claim is considered from the viewpoint of authorization. With the loosening of restrictions on the payment of benefit this authorization has necessarily to a large extent become a mere formality. But in spite of the degradation of unemployment insurance the machinery for checking up on claimants has been kept in operation.

[1] General occupations are given a code number, additional digits explaining subdivisions within the occupation. Thus 044 is the code number for a fitter or erecter; 0441 represents a worker with experience as a foreman in this occupation; and 04430 denotes a locomotive fitter.
[2] Cf. p. 14.

Where the applicant has worked in an insured trade reference is made to the Claims and Records Office of the Ministry of Labor at Kew for particulars of unexhausted contributions paid while in work (form U. I. A. 461). In the absence of such evidence the case is considered as "uncovenanted benefit." The applicant completes a form (U. I. A. 496) showing the extent of his employment since December 31, 1919. Reference is then made to his past employers for verification of the date of employment. It will be remembered that employment for "a reasonable length of time," which vague qualification might be waived in the case of ex-service men, was all that was requisite for eligibility to uncovenanted benefit under the Acts of 1922.

For those claimants who owe their eligibility to benefit to paid-up contributions, payment is authorized on receipt of confirmation from the Claims and Records Office, the principal function of which is to have available at all times the "contribution and benefit" account of each insured person. For the cases of "uncovenanted" applicants, a class which increased enormously as the depression period progressed, a different procedure is followed. These cases are provisionally authorized for payment subject to confirmation by the local Employment Committee, to which all doubtful cases should be referred before uncovenanted benefit is actually paid out.

## LOCAL EMPLOYMENT COMMITTEES

Each local Employment Committee, which works through smaller sub-committees known as "Rotas," is composed of equal numbers of representatives of employers and employed in the district covered by the Exchange. The Chairman is an appointee of the Minister of Labor, selected on the ground of local standing and a reputation for impartiality as between employers and employed. The committees are supposed to keep in close touch with the local Board of Guardians and private relief agencies, coöpting members from these agencies, in order to prevent overlapping in unemployment relief. Applicants attend personally before this committee to produce evidence in support of their claims, and are there examined by the committee members, who possess the immense asset of thorough familiarity with the current industrial situation in the district, from both the employers' and the workers' standpoint. Efforts are always made to secure the presence of a woman member when women's claims are dealt with. On the whole it may be said that no part of the unemployment insurance program has worked out to such complete satisfaction as this unpaid, volunteer service of the local Employment Committees. In all parts of the country, from all sources, tribute is paid to the value, disinterestedness, and efficiency of their work in reviewing the innumerable cases of claimants for uncovenanted benefit.[1] Experience has taught these committees to pass the *bona fide* claimant with a minimum of delay, and to check and catch the industrial slacker almost unerringly, whether or not documentary evidence of the applicant's efforts to obtain work independently of Employment Exchange facilities is demanded. There can be no doubt that the work of this part of the unemployment insurance machinery is invaluable, calling forth as it does the best of community spirit and intelligence. The drawback is that it is not insurance but doles, which the local Employment Committees supervise in examining claimants to uncovenanted benefit.

Before leaving the subject of claims to benefit it is worth noting that they are filed at the Employment Exchange in three distinct sections:

(1) Authorized claims, on which payments are due.

[1] Between March, 1921, and July, 1923, the local Employment Committees dealt with about 11,000,000 claims. Special officers from Divisional Headquarters check samples of the claims allowed. It does not appear that one per cent of those so investigated are ultimately disallowed.

(2) Straightforward claims, awaiting formal authorization.

(3) Questionable claims, on which further inquiry will precede authorization.

## REGULATIONS REGARDING BENEFIT

The unemployed worker who is entitled to benefit may without prejudice to its payment occupy himself in part-time employment[1] while waiting reference to work, or while looking for it on his own account; *provided* (a) that he is at all times available for regular employment which may offer; (b) that he can show he carried on such part-time work while in employment before; (c) that he receives from it less than from the unemployment benefit. The important feature of this regulation is its recognition of the responsibility of the Employment Exchanges as labor-placing agencies. It assumes something which should be but is not the case — that the Exchanges have knowledge of practically all vacancies existing in their respective localities at a given time. Many workers have undoubtedly been only too glad to shift the onus of finding employment on to the shoulders of the Exchanges without caring whether they have in fact achieved the effective organization of the "labor market" which is assumed.

Admittedly there has been much evasion by benefit recipients of the provisions noted above, aside from the cases where those in receipt of unemployment benefit appeal more or less directly to public charity as street vendors, itinerant musicians, pavement artists, or downright beggars. The primary safeguard, but one by no means watertight, is to have the recipient register daily at the Exchange during ordinary working hours. Suspicious cases are further investigated by officers specially appointed for this work, and in such cases benefit recipi-

[1] "Part-time employment" in the sense of odd jobs is meant. It is not to be confused with systematized "short-time" employment.

ents are often required to sign more frequently, and at varied hours.

On pay-days the applicant who has proved title to benefit attends at the appointed time. His (or her) claim is traced and the signature compared with that on the original claim form. The receipt coupon being signed, payment is made by the Pay Clerk. Benefit payments are checked within the Exchange by an ingenious triple computation which effectively prevents any internal fraud. The benefit recipient brings a receipt signed by clerk A to the Pay Clerk, who checks it from a return made by clerk B, who has had nothing to do with the authorization of claims. The need for such safeguards may be seen in the fact that many Exchanges paid out £4,000 a week, and more, in benefit for long stretches during the depression period.

As has been observed, the applicant supplies the Exchange with particulars of his industrial experience at the time of first registration. The unemployed register cannot be signed by any applicant, in respect of whom a "possible" vacancy has been notified, until he has been interviewed in the Vacancy Section, and the applicant must immediately investigate any openings to which he is directed during the period in which he draws benefit. A refusal to accept apparently suitable employment results in the immediate suspension of benefit pending decision of the Court of Referees as to the justification of this action. If the court holds it unjustified, benefit is stopped for a period not exceeding six weeks. Unemployed workers must always report back to the Vacancy Section when the position to which they have been directed has not been secured. Thus it may be ascertained whether the failure to secure employment was due to causes over which the applicant had no control.

PLACING PROCEDURE

The foregoing description of the routine in a typical Exchange does not go into the procedure of placing the registered unemployed. This part of the activity of the Exchanges is straightforward, and is still much the same as that laid down when the Labor Exchanges Act went into operation on February 1, 1910. In essence the employment work of the Exchanges, statistical activities aside, consists of four divisions.

The first of these is registration, which is compulsory for all applicants for unemployment benefit. In registering, applicants are expected to give complete details of their industrial qualifications, which information is regarded as strictly confidential. The second division is the recording, also with full details, of the vacancies notified to the Exchanges by employers. This notification of vacancies is entirely voluntary on the part of the employer, although each Exchange keeps a register of all substantial employers in its area, and is supposed to do its utmost to obtain the patronage of these local employers.

The third division is the matching of vacancies with registrations, readily accomplished by using the device of the occupational code in both cases. The fourth division is the selection and forwarding of applicants to employers who have vacancies listed, together with introductory cards which contain a space for the employer to signify whether or not the applicant has been engaged, these cards being franked for mailing back to the Exchange. It is entirely optional with both employer and applicant as to whether employment shall be entered upon after they have been brought together through the agency of the Exchange. As has been noted, however, a refusal to accept employment to which he has been directed subjects the applicant to stoppage of unemployment benefit unless he can show valid excuse. But without prejudice to continuation of benefit an applicant is entitled to decline:

(1) An offer of employment in a situation vacant in consequence of a stoppage of work due to a trade dispute.

(2) An offer of employment in the district where he was last ordinarily employed at a rate of wage lower, or on conditions

less favorable, than those which he habitually obtained in his usual employment in that district, or would have obtained had he continued to be so employed.

(3) An offer of employment in any other district at a rate of wage lower, or on conditions less favorable, than those generally observed in that district by agreement between associations of employers and of employees, or, failing any such agreement, than those generally recognized in that district by good employers.[1]

## Labor Clearing

Even in the briefest survey of the employment work of the Exchanges some mention must be made of the procedure in moving labor over the country to fill vacancies which cannot be met locally. This process is known as "Labor Clearing."

For the better execution of employment management, Great Britain has been divided into seven areas termed "Divisions," each of them in charge of a Divisional Controller who is subject to the General Manager of the Employment Exchanges, with offices at the Ministry of Labor in London. Each Divisional Controller has his headquarters at a convenient center in his area. At these Divisional Headquarters, and in a few cases at certain Exchanges in the area as well, there are established what are known as Receiving Offices for the purpose of Labor Clearing. These Receiving Offices integrate with the National Clearing House at the Ministry of Labor in London just as the Divisional Offices integrate with that of the General Manager.

When an Exchange receives a suitable vacancy which cannot be filled from its own registration of unemployed, it is the duty of the local manager first to approach his neighboring Exchanges, and if unsuccessful in obtaining an applicant therefrom to telephone particulars of the vacancy forthwith to the Receiving Office. By this office such vacancies are *either* circulated in printed lists going to all Exchanges within the area, *or* are circulated in the

[1] Unemployment Insurance Act, 1920, Section 7.

*National Clearing House Gazette* [1] to every Exchange in the country. Generally speaking, only permanent occupations, relatively well paid, which appear unlikely to be filled promptly within the district covered by the particular Receiving Office, are given national circulation. Opportunities for employment abroad, for the most part within the Empire, are frequently circulated in the *National Clearing House Gazette.* Like the *Receiving Area List,* this publication is issued every Friday, and is kept up to date by daily supplements containing cancellations and additional vacancies. Each week's issue supersedes all previous lists.

To enable work-people to take up employment found for them in other districts by the Exchanges, warrants for railway tickets are provided on the undertaking of either the worker or his new employer to repay the sum involved. By the Act of 1920 one half of the amount by which the fare exceeds four shillings may be paid out of the Unemployment Fund. In the period, less than eighteen months, from the Armistice to April 30, 1920, fares within the United Kingdom were advanced in 92,334 cases, representing an amount of £47,214.[2] But during the depression period this transference of labor fell off very markedly, due, apparently, to the fact that few occupations anywhere in Great Britain were not affected by the slump. From November, 1920, to June, 1923, only 22,606 advances were issued, to the value of £15,235; of this amount £3,300 being charged to the Unemployment Fund. As the manager of one Employment Exchange summarized it to the author: "If an order couldn't be filled in the local area, it probably meant there was something suspicious about it."

### COÖPERATION OF EMPLOYERS AND TRADE UNIONS

In a system where utilization of the Employment Exchanges by employers is entirely a voluntary matter,

---

[1] A specimen sheet of the *National Clearing House Gazette* is given in Appendix IV.

[2] Over a period of seven years unrecovered advances averaged only one half of one per cent.

success will be largely determined by the extent of employers' coöperation. There is ample evidence that to a very unfortunate degree this coöperation is lacking in Great Britain. At different times during the year 1922, a number of the managers of Exchanges were asked by the writer as to employers' coöperation in their districts. One stated that it is "on the whole very poor"; another that "while there is no active hostility, the vacancies that occur are frequently not notified to the Exchanges"; a third manager observed that "we comparatively seldom get word of the better class of vacancies." With a few striking exceptions testimony from the other managers interviewed was similar. Obviously a condition of this sort has the tendency to grow worse the longer it continues. When demand is restricted to poorer grades supply will also become restricted to inferior quality. Let enough time elapse as matters stand and the Exchanges will inevitably be still less able to provide the right men for skilled work when they are called for.

The reasons for the aloofness of many employers are complex. To some extent it appears to be due to mere inertia, ignorance of the part the Exchanges are designed to play, and a hereditary distrust of socialistic enterprise by the State. This distrust has undoubtedly been strengthened by vicious, exaggerated, and sometimes entirely false charges brought by a section of the press. It is worth noting in this connection that Mr. Alexander Thompson, "special Labor Representative" of the London *Daily Mail*, declined, on the ground that his "information rested upon hearsay only," to give evidence before the official Committee of Enquiry on Employment Exchanges which sat in the summer and autumn of 1920; while Mr. Harold Cox, another active newspaper critic, was said by this Committee to be unable to give data on which his charges could be examined.[1] Unfounded attacks on the Exchanges by certain newspapers have undoubtedly helped to hamper

[1] Cmd. 1054 (1920), pp. 5 and 7.

their work by alienating employers and the public in general. Not without reason it is asserted that attacks by the press are in part inspired by decrease in the number of "help wanted" advertisements consequent to the establishment of a national system of free, public Employment Exchanges.

One important reason for the failure of many employers to coöperate is undoubtedly found in past experiences where the Exchanges have failed to furnish the type of labor required, or where the applicants sent have proved unsatisfactory. Of greater influence during the depression period was the fact that the employer found it less easy to beat down wages for applicants forwarded from the Exchanges. In one working-class London borough the author found the opinion prevalent that "Labor wants to run the Exchange," and here for some time only one employer was serving on the local Employment Committee. Such suspicions are ridiculous. The Exchanges are Government agencies, subject to uniform Government regulations, and not in any way at the disposal of the prevalent opinion of the locality. At this particular Exchange there was something approaching an unorganized boycott by employers on the ground that policy was too radical. In a near-by district the identical policy was regarded by the local Unemployed Committee as too conservative, and effort was made to boycott the Exchange from the labor side. In the stormy waters between this Scylla and Charybdis the work of the Exchanges suffers.

Particularly in the highly skilled and better organized trades there is a tendency for the employer to take on the men he requires through local trade-union branches, without considering the Employment Exchange at all. Several factors combine to perpetuate this arrangement in the well-organized trades: (a) the existence of formal or informal agreements between employer and union to allow the latter to handle supply of the employer's requirements. Such agreements are a patent source of strength to the unions which they would sacrifice most unwillingly without due compensation. (b) The fact that, with such notable exceptions as the Tavistock Street Exchange (for the London building trades), there is so little specialization in the Exchanges. Until the organization has been considerably developed with reference to skilled workers, neither the employer who wants a specially qualified man, nor the skilled unemployed himself, will prefer the Employment Exchanges to existing trade-union arrangements. (c) The interests of the foreman run counter to utilization of the Exchanges when, as not infrequently happens, certain perquisites accrue to him from his power of hiring whomsoever he selects. And in a number of larger firms much of the authority to take on labor is vested with the foremen.

Under the Unemployment Insurance Acts practically the whole industrial population, excepting those employed in agriculture and private domestic service, must, in order to receive benefit, be registered at the Exchanges and have their Unemployment Books lodged there while out of work. Section 17 of the Act of 1920, as qualified and amended by the two Unemployment Insurance Acts of 1921, provides that the payment of benefit may be made from approved trade unions, the Government reimbursing such sums. While this improves the general coöperation between the trade-union branches and the local Employment Exchanges, it also has the result of helping to further the dissociation of the skilled worker from the Exchange, with a tendency to limit the placing work of these agencies to less skilled labor.

These factors help to check spontaneous utilization of the Exchanges by either party in the better-organized trades.

### OTHER FACTORS HAMPERING EXCHANGE EFFICIENCY

Unpleasant and inadequate premises, almost always built for another purpose and situated without regard to the industrial configuration of the district, are another manifest obstacle to Employment Exchange efficiency. In the London Borough of Stepney, as already described, the adult Exchange is on the very edge of the district served and occupies a building designed for and formerly used as a clothing warehouse. Such premises inevitably hamper efficiency on the part of the official staff. But the evil does not stop there. The more progressive the employer the less likely he is to be anxious to coöperate with a Government agency which seems of so little importance that its offices can be shoved into any old building which happens to be available at a low rent. Nor is the Stepney Exchange below the average in housing. For the Boroughs of Shoreditch and Bethnal Green the Employment Exchange in 1922 occupied a small group of old, unpainted army huts, located in a sort of yard, reached by an alleyway from a relatively unimportant street. In the Borough of Poplar, Exchange accommodations, in a former German seamen's home, are so cramped that to have a special room for dock laborers they have had to be put in the basement. The situation in the great cities of the provinces is generally little better. Employers who have examined the premises to which the Employment Exchanges are too often relegated are justified in being skeptical as to the value of their service.[1]

The employer can transact his business with the Exchange by telephone or letter. But the unemployed worker must turn up there regularly to sign the register. In doing so he or she literally rubs shoulders with hundreds of the lowest type of unskilled and casual — a type that always predominates for the reason that no provision is made for them elsewhere, as is the case with well-organized trade unionists. The odor in the public rooms of the Exchanges when crowded is often most offensive, and the dirt accumulated is such that a thorough fumigation has to be frequently carried out. On the whole it is not remarkable that

[1] See, also, what is said on the subject of unsatisfactory premises in Cmd. 1054 (1920), p. 14.

the more self-respecting workers often shun the Exchanges as long as possible, and that some few even prefer to sacrifice the insurance which they have compulsorily paid rather than go through the ordeal of constant contact with such unpleasant surroundings.

After the obstacle of improper premises comes the competition which is given by newspaper advertising, gate-hiring, and private fee-charging employment agencies. The licenses of the latter are now strictly controlled by the municipal governments, and their competition, except perhaps in the case of domestic servants, is not material. Gate-hiring, of course, cuts into the work of the Exchanges to a considerable extent. Newspaper advertising, instead of utilization of the Exchange facilities, is a more serious obstacle and by helping to limit the number of vacancies reported to the Exchanges materially lessens their success as placing agencies. And the less their success as placing agencies the more the Exchanges tend to fall into disrepute.

The very harmful effect of unemployment insurance on placing work is discussed in the following chapter.

### COMPULSORY REGISTRATION OF VACANCIES

Under present conditions the question of making it compulsory for employers to notify all their vacancies to the Exchanges is somewhat theoretical. Manifestly there would have to be considerable improvements before a step of such magnitude could be successfully carried through. But several points indicate the stage has now been reached where this step must be seriously considered.

(a) Employment Exchange operation at the present time is bound in a vicious circle. Until there is better coöperation from employers in notifying vacancies the service cannot be greatly improved. At least until the service is improved many employers will not notify vacancies. Even then experience gives no ground for belief that universal and whole-hearted coöperation will be given voluntarily.

(b) The present condition lends itself to fraud and extravagance, inasmuch as the Exchange must pay regular benefits to the qualified unemployed worker without having the facilities for finding him employment which compulsory notification would give. Means for providing that the insurance recipient shall in every case be a *bona fide* work-seeker are, and under existing arrangements must be, inadequate.

(c) Compulsory registration of vacancies would not necessarily preclude the employer from taking on workers in any other way he sees fit. It would mean that the Exchanges would have a more certain knowledge of the state of the employment market, and would be able to handle the payment of unemployment relief with more justice and efficiency.

(d) It was considered essential to make all insured work-people lodge their unemployment books with the Exchanges on falling out of work. *Prima facie* there is no reason to hold that to compel employers to register their vacancies in like manner would be a step of any greater social severity.

## REFUSALS TO FILL VACANCIES OFFERED

Except for valid reasons very few unemployed men refuse to accept vacancies to which they are forwarded by the Exchanges. Refusals are more common with women. While the reason for this has not been fully analyzed, it appears to be partly due to the inferiority of women's wages, and partly to the fact that women whose husbands, fathers, or brothers are at work do not feel economic pressure so keenly that they are forced to take any work without some discrimination of their own. Among male bread-winners conditions of the depression period have almost completely broken down this disposition to choose, except in the case of work as strike-breakers. Many men accepted work at pay below union rates, even though a refusal on this score is not followed by benefit disqualification.

In this connection is to be noted a most dangerous procedure developed by a few employers during the depression. This is an attempt to utilize the Exchanges to break down trade-union standards. It has been pointed out that the Exchanges are chiefly relied on by the more poorly organized workers. With this class of unemployed a not uncommon occurrence is for an employer, when notifying a vacancy to the Exchange, to evade stating the wages he proposes to pay. When an applicant is forwarded this type of employer then carefully "sounds him out" until it has been ascertained whether or not the worker is willing to be engaged at a figure below the standard rate. If the applicant refuses, a pretext for unsuitability is easily forthcoming, and when the Exchange inquires the reason for rejection this pretext is given — "too old," "too young," "insolent," "timid," or perhaps just a general "not suitable." The order is then placed again with the Exchange and the procedure continues until a man comes along sufficiently needy and despairing to accept whatever pittance is offered.

The policy of strict neutrality in cases of strikes and lock-outs is very successfully maintained by the Exchanges. When notifications of vacancies due to these causes come in from employers, full information of the circumstances is given to applicants in the Vacancy Section. There is no benefit disqualification for refusing such openings offhand. The testimony of a large number of Employment Exchange managers justifies the estimate that in spite of the depression there are not more than one or two cases in a hundred where an unemployed worker uses the Exchanges to take a job offered by reason of an industrial dispute.

# CHAPTER IX

## THE BURDEN ON THE EXCHANGES

THE appalling complexity of State-operated unemployment insurance development during the depression period; its "uncovenanted benefits," "special periods," "gap periods," changes in amount of contributions and benefits, and many other irritating, short-lived shifts in procedure have been traced in some detail in this study. In the last chapter a survey of the work of the Employment Exchanges was given, together with some comment on general difficulties encountered in their operation. The road is now clear for an examination of the effect on placing work of its subordination to the operation of unemployment insurance. More than any other single obstacle it is probable that this mistaken view of what is the primary function of the Employment Exchanges has hampered their efficacy as job-finding agencies.

The official opinion that the Employment Exchanges were established "not solely or even mainly as placing agencies, but in order to prepare a machinery for the administration of unemployment insurance," has already been noted.[1] In spite of a maze of complicated legislation on the subject, the Exchanges during the depression period successfully fulfilled their multitudinous duties as insurance offices. Placing work, being regarded by the Government as secondary, has necessarily been treated as secondary to insurance. Unemployed workers have been excused from signing the register and excused from regular attendance in search of work. If the efficiency and reputation of the Exchanges as placing agencies have suffered as a result of pressure and consequent relaxations, it is the

[1] See p. 9.

fault of the system and not of the staff. To what extent
placing work has suffered, and at what enormous cost of
human energy the unemployment insurance program of
the Government has been carried on, it is the purpose
of this chapter to consider.

TABLE IX. PLACING WORK OF THE EMPLOYMENT EXCHANGES[1]

| YEAR | REGISTRA-TIONS | INDIVIDUALS REGISTERED | VACANCIES NOTIFIED | VACANCIES FILLED | INDIVIDUALS PLACED |
|---|---|---|---|---|---|
| 1911 | 1,965,991 | Not available | 769,661 | 608,475 | Not available |
| 1912 | 2,362,225 | Not available | 1,033,780 | 809,553 | Not available |
| 1913 | 2,836,366 | 1,783,951 | 1,183,356 | 895,273 | 632,666 |
| 1914 | 3,442,452 | 2,164,023 | 1,479,024 | 1,116,909 | 814,071 |
| 1915 | 3,186,137 | 2,326,803 | 1,797,646 | 1,308,137 | 1,058,336 |
| 1916 | 3,658,689 | 2,843,784 | 2,049,018 | 1,557,235 | 1,351,406 |
| 1917 | 3,575,380 | 2,837,650 | 1,999,442 | 1,555,223 | 1,375,198 |
| 1918 | 3,739,064 | 3,045,263 | 2,067,217 | 1,514,712 | 1,324,743 |
| 1919 | 6,197,653 | 5,003,786 | 1,951,364 | 1,289,963 | 1,137,875 |
| 1920 | 4,570,898 | 3,492,596 | 1,312,133 | 941,708 | 784,169 |
| 1921 | 9,303,526 | 6,548,867 | 1,024,602 | 842,462 | 716,841 |
| 1922 | 7,131,294a | Not available | 860,692 | 724,783 | Not available |
| 1923 | 7,261,018b | Not available | 1,027,831 | 885,422 | Not available |

a Registrations for 1922 are for the period from January 10, 1922, to January 8, 1923,
and are therefore subject to slight revision for the calendar year.
b Registrations for 1923 are for the period from January 8, 1923 to January 7, 1924.
"Vacancies notified" for this year is subject to a very small upward revision.

DECREASE IN UTILIZATION BY EMPLOYERS

Table IX, giving the main features of the placing work
of the Employment Exchanges from their establishment
to the close of 1923, is interesting, but does not provide a
basis for any very definite conclusions. The marked increase
in registrations is due primarily to the widening application
of compulsion through successive Unemployment Insurance
Acts.[2] The decline from 1918 to 1923 in vacancies notified
is a better subject for analysis as notification is a matter

[1] Exclusive of casual labor placements.
[2] The abnormal increase of registrations in 1919 and 1921 is noteworthy. In 1919 it is in part attributable to the effect of Out-of-Work
Donations (cf. Table II, p. 32). That of 1921 is in part attributable
to the re-registration, at the outset of Special Benefit Periods, of work-
people who had allowed their applications for work at the Employment
Exchanges to lapse. (See Chapter X on "Unemployment Statistics,"
especially pp. 129–131.

which is optional with the individual employer. To some extent, of course, this decline is due to the fact that during the depression period there were fewer vacancies to notify. But this does not account for the fact that while unemployment did not begin to become serious until the very end of 1920,[1] the drop in notified vacancies began with the end of the war and was sharper during the post-war period of good employment than after the depression had set in. What applies to vacancies notified to the Exchanges is, naturally enough, applicable to the statistics of vacancies filled by the Exchanges. Obviously many employers were not utilizing the Employment Exchanges during 1919 and 1920.

Assertion that the continued drop in vacancies notified during 1921 and 1922 was also in part due to lack of utilization of the Exchanges by employers may seem, at first glance, far-fetched. Assuredly, one feels, the trade depression, meaning fewer vacancies, amply explains the falling off in 1921 and 1922. But the mere fact that the drop from each preceding year was 639,231 in 1920; 287,531 in 1921; and 163,910 in 1922, with a rise to the level of two years previous in 1923, gives basis for belief that something more than the curtailment of jobs was at issue here during the depression period.

By the end of 1920 the Exchanges had completed ten full years of operation, and had to their credit a deserved reputation for the effective performance of vital work during the war.[2] In 1920 there were 395 Exchanges in operation as against 225 in 1911. In 1911 employment was on the whole somewhat worse than in 1920, the mean trade-union percentage of unemployment being 3.0 in the former year as against 2.4 in the latter. Yet the number of va-

[1] The mean trade-union percentage of unemployment for 1920 was 2.4. For the last four months of the year it was respectively 2.2, 5.3, 3.7, and 6.1.

[2] A clear, though very brief, summary of special work handled by the Exchanges during the war is found in Cmd. 1140 (1921), pp. 12 and 13.

cancies notified to the Exchanges in 1920 was well under twice the figure for 1911, was only eleven per cent above that for 1913, and was considerably below the number for 1914.

The suspicion arises that the check in the rate of decline in vacancy notifications during the depression period may be partly attributable to a post-war withdrawal of their voluntary patronage by many employers. While impossible of proof, the argument is justified by the opinion of many Employment Exchange managers that the complexities of unemployment insurance operation have seriously harmed the reputation of Exchanges as placing agencies, and caused the alienation of a number of employers who, when placing work was still most emphasized, were glad to report their vacancies. Such inquisitorial adjuncts of State-operated unemployment insurance as the visits of inspectors to establishments to verify due payment of contributions have caused a very real undercurrent of irritation among employers, though something has been done to minimize this annoyance since 1921 by having one set of inspectors investigate for both health and unemployment insurance.

## EFFICIENCY OF PLACING WORK DURING DEPRESSION

Whether avertible or not, the decline in the notification of vacancies is the more to be lamented because the Exchanges actually, though not relatively, stood during the depression period on a higher level of efficiency than at any previous time. This is brought out by Table X, which shows for each complete year of Employment Exchange operation the proportion of registrations transformed into jobs and the proportion of notified vacancies filled. The percentage of vacancies filled by the Exchanges in each year is obviously a fair general test of whether they have improved the efficiency of their placing work during the period under survey.

TABLE X.  PROPORTION OF REGISTRATIONS AND VACANCIES
          FILLED

| YEAR | REGISTRATIONS FILLED (Per cent) | NOTIFIED VACANCIES FILLED (Per cent) |
|------|------|------|
| 1911 . . . . . . . . | 31.0 | 79.1 |
| 1912 . . . . . . . . | 34.3 | 78.3 |
| 1913 . . . . . . . . | 31.6 | 75.7 |
| 1914 . . . . . . . . | 32.4 | 75.5 |
| 1915 . . . . . . . . | 41.1 | 72.8 |
| 1916 . . . . . . . . | 42.6 | 76.0 |
| 1917 . . . . . . . . | 43.5 | 77.8 |
| 1918 . . . . . . . . | 40.5 | 73.3 |
| 1919 . . . . . . . . | 20.8 | 66.1 |
| 1920 . . . . . . . . | 20.6 | 71.8 |
| 1921 . . . . . . . . | 9.1 | 82.2 |
| 1922 . . . . . . . . | 10.2 | 84.2 |
| 1923 . . . . . . . . | 12.2 | 86.1a |

a Subject to downward revision of a small fraction of one per cent.

From this Table it is seen that the percentages of notified vacancies filled by the Exchanges during the depression years 1921, 1922, and 1923 were higher than in any of the preceding years. Some increase in this percentage would be expected, from the fact that the available supply was so much greater. The gain, however, is so marked that it is impossible to argue there has been retrogression in the ability of the Exchanges to fill vacancies. Nor is this the only evidence that the placing work of the Exchanges has been kept as effective as ever. The extension of compulsory registration and the decline in vacancies notified to the Exchanges has naturally resulted in the proportion of registrations filled being low in the post-war years. But further examination will show that the fall is no reflection on the placing work of the Exchanges. The mean annual average number of registrations for the pre-war years 1911, 1912, and 1913 was 2,388,194; for the depression years 1921, 1922, and 1923 it was 7,898,613. The ratio of increase in registrations was therefore 3.32. The average percentage of registrations converted into jobs for the period 1911–13 was 32.3 and for 1921–23, 10.5. The ratio of decrease in what may be called consummated registrations was therefore 3.08. The fact that registrations converted into jobs decreased by a somewhat lesser ratio than the registrations themselves increased is also good evidence that the placing work of the Exchanges has not deteriorated in quality.

## INCREASE OF STAFF WITH UNEMPLOYMENT INSURANCE

But the analysis so far has given no consideration to the expenditure of energy involved in keeping the placing work of the Exchanges at pre-war level. Just as the number of hours worked has to be considered in making wage comparisons, so other factors must be taken into account in this effort to observe the effect of unemployment insurance on Employment Exchange operation. Important among these is the relative size of the staffs which achieved, as we have seen, approximately equal placing results in 1911–13 and 1921–23. For this we turn to Table XI, giving the staff at work in the entire Employment Exchange organization at March 31st of every year since 1910, the proportion of vacancies filled in each year for each member of the staff, and other relevant statistics.

TABLE XI.  PLACING WORK IN PROPORTION TO EMPLOYMENT EXCHANGE PERSONNEL

| YEAR | On March 31, each year | | VACANCIES FILLED | YEARLY PLACEMENTS PER STAFF MEMBER | MEAN TRADE UNION PERCENTAGE UNEMPLOYMENT |
| | EXCHANGES OPEN [a] | TOTAL STAFF | | | |
|---|---|---|---|---|---|
| 1911 | 225 | 1,002 | 608,475 | 607 | 3.0 |
| 1912 | 414 | 1,481 | 809,553 | 547 | 3.2 |
| 1913 | 412 | 4,861 | 895,273 | 184 | 2.1 |
| 1914 | 413 | 5,250 | 1,116,909 | 213 | 3.3 |
| 1915 | 383 | 4,789 | 1,308,137 | 273 | 1.1 |
| 1916 | 372 | 4,784 | 1,557,235 | 326 | 0.4 |
| 1917 | 356 | 5,662 | 1,555,223 | 275 | 0.7 |
| 1918 | 357 | 6,342 | 1,514,712 | 239 | 0.8 |
| 1919 | 392 | 19,384b | 1,289,963 | 67 | 2.4 |
| 1920 | 395 | 13,204 | 941,708 | 71 | 2.4 |
| 1921 | 394 | 14,500c | 842,462 | 58c | 15.3 |
| 1922 | 390 | 11,100c | 724,783 | 65c | 15.4 |
| 1923 | 385 | 9,200c | 885,422 | 96c | 11.5 |

a Exclusive of Branch Employment Offices.

b Abnormal increase due to O.W.D. and other temporary work arising after Armistice.

c Staff figures for years 1921-22-23 fluctuated sharply from month to month, temporary clerks being hired and dismissed in large numbers as the demands of the unemployment insurance program varied. The figures given as of March 31 in these three years are not the actual numbers of the staff employed on those particular dates, but a close estimate of the mean for the respective years. Numbers employed in the Claims and Record Office at Kew, and at Branch Employment offices, are not included in staff figures for these three years.

The material presented in Table XI merits careful analysis. We may notice first that the relation between the degree of unemployment and the number of placements made by the Exchanges is much less direct than might have been expected. For instance, in 1920 as a whole employment was very good. In 1921 it was phenomenally bad. Yet the downward variation between 1920 and 1921 in the number of vacancies filled is scarcely more than the upward variation between 1912 and 1913, although unemployment varied 12.9 per cent in the first case and 1.1 per cent in the second. Obviously unemployment is not the only factor entering into the number of vacancies filled by the Exchanges. This negative conclusion, however, is of small assistance except as it helps to verify the argument that the placing work of the Exchanges has been on a high level of efficiency during the depression period, even though they were less utilized by employers.

More to the point is the amazing evidence brought out by this table as to the disproportionate energy which has been directed into the operation of unemployment insurance. On March 31, 1912, before the first Unemployment Insurance Act went into operation, the placing work of 414 Exchanges, together with all the duties of Divisional and Headquarters offices, was handled by a total staff of 1481. Between that date and January, 1922, when the total staff employed numbered 13,732, the number of Employment Exchanges was slightly reduced and very little change was made in the procedure of job finding and placing. Throughout 1922, even after serious and successful effort had been made by the Government to bring about reductions in personnel,[1] the staff showed a nearly eight-fold increase, to the average number of over 11,000. When every excuse has been made, the glaring

---

[1] In July, 1921, at the peak of unemployment, the staff numbered 20,288. By July, 1923, it had been reduced to 9132, of whom 4180 were permanent and 4952 temporary. The great majority of the male employees are ex-service men and about one quarter of them are disabled.

fact remains that a staff averaging over 11,000 in 1922 placed fewer unemployed than a staff of 1500 in 1912. Or again, in 1923, with the heaviest pressure for economy and efficiency, nearly twice the staff as compared with 1913 made 10,000 fewer placements. And in these comparisons (as noted in footnote c to Table XI) staff figures for 1921–23 do not include the hundreds of clerical workers at the Claims and Record office.

Testifying in June, 1920, before the Committee of Enquiry into the Work of the Employment Exchanges Mr. T. W. Phillips, Principal Assistant Secretary, Ministry of Labor, stated that the operation of both unemployment insurance and ordinary Employment Exchange work "is done by the same staff as a rule, and in the same office." [1] But in spite of the constant assertion by the Ministry of Labor that it is impossible to differentiate between that part of the personnel engaged in straight employment work and those whose energies are occupied by unemployment insurance, it appears from the above figures that a rough ratio among the total staff can be drawn. And the evidence is that this grossly disproportionate ratio works out at approximately seven engaged on unemployment insurance to one on straight employment work. The inference is that should unemployment insurance cease to be a State function, seven eighths of the Employment Exchange staff could be dispensed with and placing work still show no ill effects.

In short, the slight improvement in the efficiency of the Exchanges which is discoverable, and which is certainly no greater than should have been expected after thirteen years of operation, has been won at a totally disproportionate increase in personnel and expense. Whereas in 1911, placements worked out at an average of 607 a year, or nearly 12 a week, for each member of the executive, administrative, clerical, and statistical staffs, in 1922 placements averaged 65 a year, or little over one a week,

[1] Cmd. 1140 (1921), p. 21.

for each member of the total staff, exclusive of those employed at the Claims and Record office. The extent of the burden of unemployment insurance on the Exchanges may be summarized by saying that an eight-fold increase in staff effected a barely perceptible improvement in the quality of their work. And any good effects in improving the reputation of the Exchanges which should have been brought by this slight improvement have been more than swept away by the myriad complications and irritations which State-operated unemployment insurance has introduced.

### THE STRAIN OF EMERGENCY LEGISLATION

To these complications the manner in which Unemployment Insurance Acts were galloped into operation during the depression period has greatly added. Insurance legislation, shown by its sequel to have been poorly planned, was not only rushed through Parliament but made immediately operative, or even retroactive, in a manner

TABLE XII.  DATES OF ENACTMENT AND OPERATION OF
UNEMPLOYMENT INSURANCE ACTS

| ACT | DATE PASSED | DATE OF OPERATION |
|---|---|---|
| Unemployment Insurance (Temporary Provisions Amendment) Act, 1920. . . . . . . . . . | Dec.   23, 1920 | Dec.   23, 1920 |
| Unemployment Insurance Act, 1921 . . . . . . . . . . . | March  3, 1921 | March  3, 1921 |
| Unemployment Insurance (No. 2) Act, 1921. . . . . . . . . | July   1, 1921 | June   30, 1921 (earliest date) |
| Unemployed Workers' Dependants' (Temporary Provision) Act, 1921 . . . . . . . . . | Nov.   8, 1921 | Nov.   10, 1921 (Nov. 7, for contributions) |
| Unemployment Insurance Act, 1922 . . . . . . . . . . . | April  12, 1922 | April   6, 1922 |
| Unemployment Insurance (No. 2) Act, 1922. . . . . . . . . | July   20, 1922 | July   20, 1922 |
| Unemployment Insurance Act, 1923 . . . . . . . . . . | March 29, 1923 | April   12, 1923 |

which caused immense confusion and waste of energy in the Exchanges. The point is illustrated by the preceding table, giving the dates on which Acts of 1921 and 1922 were actually passed, and the dates on which they came into operation.

The overtime worked by the Employment Exchange staffs as a direct result of the inadequate preparation for these Acts has been ascertained for a few sample weeks. In two weeks after the passage of the Act of December, 1920 (a relatively unimportant Act), 231,500 hours of overtime were worked. In three weeks after the passage of the Act of March, 1921, over 300,000 hours. In the first week after the passage of the Act of July, 1921, 147,000 hours. Nor was this disconcerting pressure limited to one, two, or three weeks after enactment. After each Act the extra strain caused by putting new and involved legislation into practice lasted for at least several weeks, so that the total overtime caused by all the Acts listed above must be reckoned in millions of hours. Add to this the inevitable mistakes made by an overworked personnel in after-office hours, and the tens of thousands of queries, each demanding investigation and answer, coming in from the Claims and Record and Divisional and Headquarters offices as these mistakes were discovered, and the wonder grows that the Exchanges should have been able to keep the placing work to as high a standard as was maintained during the depression period.

Particularly illuminating was the experience at the time of the Act of April, 1922, which went into operation six days before it became law! Due to inevitable ignorance at Employment Exchange Headquarters as to what the final provisions of this Act would be, no less than five circulars, giving tentative instructions, were sent to local Exchanges on March 29 and April 3, 6, 7, and 8. These were succeeded and superseded by a 31-page circular on April 13, these instructions in turn being followed by new ones when three months later the Act of July, 1922, came over the horizon. The reader who has struggled through the simplified summaries of the depression period Acts given in Chapter V will be able to gather some idea of the feelings of the managers of the Employment Exchanges, called upon to assimilate and put in operation extremely complicated instructions which were scarcely mastered before a new Act brought in its new flood of literature from the central office.

### EXCESSIVE ACCOUNTING

Among the many minor complications of the unemployment insurance program may be mentioned two which have come under adverse criticism by the Inter-Departmental Committee appointed in January, 1922, "to consider the relations of health insurance and unemployment insurance." One of these is the provision of the 1920 Act restricting unemployment benefit (except, of course, uncovenanted benefit) to one week for every six of contribution. The other complication is the provision of this Act entitling insured persons who reach the age of sixty to a refund of the excess of their contributions over the amount of benefit received, plus compound interest at two and one half per cent.

These devices have required the continuous maintenance of a separate ledger account for each insured person and have been found to involve an "excessive burden of accounting." The refund system, which combines the characteristics of State banking with those of insurance, has been a particularly heavy burden on the Exchanges considering the very questionable value of the scheme.[1] In April, 1924, the Labor Government proposed doing away with these refunds altogether.

In Great Britain the true function of Employment Exchanges — which, to reiterate, is to bring together the suitable unemployed worker and the appropriate

[1] See Cmd. 1821 of 1923. *Third Interim Report of Inter-Departmental Committee.*

vacant job with the greatest possible saving of time and energy — has been obscured and interfered with by the imposition of State-operated unemployment insurance. It should, therefore, be of service very briefly to summarize German post-war experience in handling unemployment relief, for in the German policy there has been one fundamental difference from the British method appreciation of which will help to summarize much that has been written in this study.

## ABSENCE OF STATE–OPERATED UNEMPLOYMENT INSURANCE IN GERMANY

In its broad basic outline the system of German Employment Exchanges (*Nachweise*) is practically identical with that of Great Britain. Local offices are linked with a district central office (*Landesarbeitsamt*) and these in turn integrate into the Federal Ministry of Labor (*Reichsarbeitsministerium*) in Berlin, much as the local Exchanges in Great Britain link with Divisional offices and these with the Ministry of Labor in London. Procedure of registration, vacancy notification, "matching" of job and registered worker, and forwarding of applicant for employment is in all essentials identical in both countries. Special functions, such as industrial training and State-aided public works programs are worked through the coöperation of the German *Nachweise* much as they are through the coöperation of the British Employment Exchanges. Juvenile employment work, carried on in coöperation with the schools, and its corollary of vocational guidance, are much the same in both countries, even down to the questionnaires filled out by pupil, parents, teachers, and school physician in the last year of compulsory schooling.

There are, of course, many variations from the general parallel. There is more specialization by industry in the German Exchanges. Their statistical work is not so com-

plete. Organized short-time as an alternative to complete
unemployment has been carried further in Germany,
largely because of pressure by the trade unions. Adult
industrial training, as a conscious attempt to organize
the direction of workers from overcrowded occupations
to industries where their services are and will probably
continue to be in demand, is in its infancy in England
compared to its development in Germany. So is the
program of "Productive Unemployment Relief" (*produktive Erwerbslosenfürsorge*)[1] which differs essentially from
what is generally understood by public "relief work"
in either Great Britain or the United States. But even
the sum of these variations is small compared with the
one major distinction in British and German method.
What that distinction is can be put in a single sentence.
*The Germans have refused to clog up their Employment
Exchange machinery with State-operated unemployment
insurance.* Where it is thought necessary, the German
Government pays an outright dole for complete unemployment, this being handled by a relatively small staff
in offices altogether distinct from those where the placing
work is operated. Fraud is guarded against quite as well
as in Great Britain by the rule that no one who cannot
bring from the Employment Exchange evidence of his
inability to get work is eligible for the dole. And it is
no more than the obvious truth to say that the experiments and developments by which the German Employment Exchanges have been able to forge ahead of the
British in several important respects, are due primarily
to the fact that they have been kept free from the burden
of operating an impossible system of unemployment insurance.

[1] A comprehensive sketch of the German post-war program of
unemployment relief is found in a series of three articles by the author
printed in the London *Nation and Athenæum* on October 22, November
5, and November 26, 1921. Because of special interest and importance
a part of the third of these articles, relating to the "Productive Unemployment Relief" program, is reprinted in Appendix V.

In Germany, in short, the Government preferred an open and outright system of doles to cluttering up its Employment Exchange machinery with a system of State-operated unemployment insurance of problematical benefit. In England, State-operated unemployment insurance was put first, and the development of the Exchanges as agencies for organizing the "labor market" was made secondary. During the post-war testing period insurance virtually degenerated to doles in Great Britain and by that very degeneration the organization of employment work was held at virtually the same level of development which it had reached before the war. But in Germany the Employment Exchange system, unhampered by insurance, was able to go ahead with constructive work.

And one may hazard the opinion that the small amount of post-war unemployment in Germany prior to the Ruhr occupation, as compared with that in Great Britain, had a contributory reason less widely heralded than that of high production costs in the latter country and the stimulus of a depreciating currency in the former. German markets have been more disturbed than those of Great Britain; essential raw materials have been as costly. But by keeping her Employment Exchange system and all its subsidiary developments free for the primary function of organizing the "labor market" Germany has been able to accomplish certain noteworthy results in the curative treatment of unemployment, which have been much more difficult of attainment in Great Britain since the day when the operation of unemployment insurance was loaded on to the Exchanges.

# CHAPTER X

## UNEMPLOYMENT STATISTICS

THERE are three separate sources of unemployment statistics in Great Britain, none of which is in itself reliable for more than general conclusions, and each of which has advantages and disadvantages not shared by the other two. The simplest index is given by the numbers remaining on the "Live Registers" of the Employment Exchanges at any given time. The more complex sources of information are found, (a) in the number of Unemployment Books belonging to members of insured industries "lodged" at the Exchanges at any given time, and, (b) in the figures of unemployment among their membership furnished monthly to the Ministry of Labor by a number of representative trade unions.

### LIVE REGISTER STATISTICS

Due to the limitations on benefit the quantitative measurement of unemployment given by the Live Register figures was often erratic and unreliable during the depression period. As unemployed work-people exhausted their rights to benefit many of them ceased to patronize the Exchanges, and thereby went off the Live Register lists even though they still remained completely unemployed. Then, when another "special period" of benefit began these unregistered unemployed, being eligible for benefit again, swarmed back to the Exchanges and again entered the statistical totals. Naturally this fluctuation was most pronounced during the early part of the depression period. As insurance degenerated towards the level of doles and restrictions on the payment of benefit became less, the number ineligible at any given time became smaller and smaller. Consequently, by the end of 1922, the Live Register figures had come to be a fairly accurate index of the total number of unemployed in insured industries, covering by far the greater part of the industrial population of Great Britain.[1]

But for many months the Live Register figures were, for statistical purposes, worthless. On June 24, 1921, at the extreme depth of the worst phase of the depression, 2,177,899 individuals were registered at the Exchanges as completely unemployed. On October 21, 1921, the number of completely unemployed on the Live Registers of the Exchanges had dropped to 1,423,792. But this apparently immense improvement was in reality largely negatived by the fact that a number officially estimated as at least 300,000 had by the later date gone off the Live Register — not because they had found employment, but because having exhausted their right to benefit under the first special period they apparently felt it wasted time to maintain registration.

This defect in the Live Register statistics was admitted at the time by the then Minister of Labor, Dr. T. J. Macnamara, in an interview published in the London *Daily Telegraph* on October 3, 1921. Observing that by September 23d benefit under the first special period had been exhausted by 519,000 unemployed, Dr. Macnamara said:

Of these 343,000 had ceased to register, presumably because there was no more benefit for them. But I must not assume that any, save a very few indeed, of these have in fact found work. The figure for the total number of persons out of work must not now be taken as 1,445,000 — the figure I gave you for September 23d — but probably much more nearly 1,750,000.

For all close observers the suspicions of Live Register inadequacy received proof as soon as the second special period of benefit became operative, on November 3, 1921. By November 11th the numbers of registered unemployed had swollen to 1,789,432. This did not mean that in the

[1] For a complete list of uninsured occupations see Appendix I.

three weeks from October 21st unemployment had suddenly come to 366,000 workers. It did mean that those who had been temporarily ineligible for benefit had, with the new special period, found it financially profitable to resume contact with the Exchanges. The same situation held as numbers of the unemployed exhausted the benefits to which they were entitled under the second special period, and generally to the complete deception of a large section of press and public. The London *Times* of March 29, 1922, for instance, cited a decrease of 30,000 in the Live Register figures between March 13th and March 20th under the heading: "Less Unemployment. Largest Week's Decrease This Year." But March 20th was less than three weeks from the date when the third special period of benefit was started, and investigation shows that a large proportion of the 30,000 decrease in that particular week was due not to any improvement in employment, but to desertion of the Exchanges by unemployed who had ceased to be eligible for benefit in the second special period.

It has been shown that as the depression continued successive Unemployment Insurance Acts made the period of eligibility for benefit more and more protracted.[1] As the condition in which "benefit" would be continuous was steadily approached, the numbers deserting the Live Registers became relatively trivial. On February 26, 1923, for instance, the number on the Live Registers was 1,376,409 and the number of Employment Books lodged 1,388,860, the discrepancy of the Live Registers from the more accurate figure (which will be discussed in the following paragraphs) being thus less than one per cent. The obvious inference from this is that if the Government had from the beginning of the depression period followed an outright policy of granting doles, instead of a policy which started as insurance and degenerated to disguised doles, the Live Register statistics of the Exchanges would have had some value. But as matters

[1] See Chapter V, and Table VIII, p. 95.

stood these statistics were virtually worthless, and the immense amount of clerical work involved in their tabulation was therefore largely wasted.

## STATISTICS BASED ON LODGED UNEMPLOYMENT BOOKS

In the Ministry of Labor itself, however, there have been no illusions as to the adequacy of the Live Register statistics in providing a quantitative measure of unemployment. A more reliable gauge is available in the total number of Unemployment Books lodged at the Exchanges by the members of insured trades who have fallen out of work. In order to receive benefit it is necessary for the insured unemployed to lodge their books, and on exhausting benefit there is no particular reason why the book should be withdrawn, especially since the whole procedure of lodging it once more must be gone through in order to entitle the owner to benefit when he has again become eligible.

Even the figure of Unemployment Books lodged at the Exchanges, however, has not proved as accurate a measure of unemployment among the twelve million insured workers as might have been expected, aside from the fact that it does not consider unemployment in uninsured occupations. During the depression period the number of unemployed who, after exhausting benefit, went off the Live Register was much greater than the number withdrawing Unemployment Books. Nevertheless, there is no doubt that the proportion in the latter class was sufficiently large to make even the more accurate figure unreliable at times. It has been mentioned that towards the close of the first special period the Live Registers failed to take into account upwards of 300,000 unemployed members of insured trades. At this time it was unofficially estimated by the statistical department of the Ministry of Labor that about one half of this number had also "lifted" their Unemployment Books, and thus temporarily disappeared altogether from all Government records of unemployment. This condition has been referred to (none too prominently) in the official Labor Gazette,[1] but is far from generally recognized. Unfortunately there is reason to believe that in making its statistics public the Ministry of Labor, during the worst of the depression period, sometimes thought more of psychological effect than of strict accuracy.

The occasional unreliability of the insured trades statistics can be noted in the table on the next two pages, comparing, for the years 1921, 1922, and 1923, the percentages of unemployment reported by those trade unions making returns to the Ministry of Labor with the percentages of unemployment among insured workers as calculated from the number of books remaining lodged at the Exchanges. The months in which the first, second, third, and fourth special periods began have been marked with an asterisk. To indicate more clearly the turning point in the postwar depression the statistics for the early months of 1924 have been included.

In the case of the second special period there is clearly shown in the second column the disproportionate jump resulting from the renewal of relations with the Exchanges by many workers who, while remaining unemployed, had previously withdrawn their books. In the case of the third and fourth special periods this unjustified diminution followed by a jump back to accuracy is barely perceptible. The chief reason for this improvement in the accuracy of the Employment Exchange statistics has already been noted. As insurance became more akin to doles and the length of benefit ineligibility lessened, fewer unemployed troubled to withdraw their vacant books. The collapse of insurance brought a progressive improvement in the value of the statistical work of the Exchanges.

[1] See, for example, the third footnote to the article on page 2 of the Labor Gazette for January, 1922.

### COMPARISON OF TRADE-UNION AND INSURED-TRADES STATISTICS

Although we shall take up next a detailed consideration of the trade-union statistics, it is well to note from Table XIII a clear reflection of their fallibility. It must be remembered that the second column in this table covers from nine to ten times as many workers as the first, and, as will be shown, the trade unions reporting are by no means a fair index of the whole industrial population. The industries of engineering and shipbuilding alone, and by no means all the workers therein, make up one third or more of the total membership on which the trade union statistics are based. At the time of the stoppage of work in the coal industry during the spring of 1921, and to a lesser extent throughout all of 1921 and 1922, these industries showed an amount of unemployment which was not reflected in the insured trades taken as a whole. This defect in the trade-union percentages is apparent in the following table:

TABLE XIII.  PERCENTAGES OF UNEMPLOYMENT IN 1921, 1922, AND 1923[1]

| MONTH (END OF) | TRADE-UNION PERCENTAGE | INSURED-TRADES PERCENTAGE[2] |
|---|---|---|
| 1921 | | |
| January | 6.9 | 8.2 |
| February | 8.5 | 9.5 |
| March | 10.0 | 11.3 |

[1] The mean averages for the three years 1921, 1922, and 1923 are: Trade-Union Percentage, 14.07; Insured-Trades Percentage, 12.851. The chart which follows should be carefully examined in connection with this table. In addition to the three years, 1921, 1922, and 1923 it affords a striking comparison of the two records of percentage unemployment from the outset of unemployment insurance. Two points are particularly noticeable: The greater regularity which the trade-union curve generally exhibits. The fact that the insured trades curve, commonly exhibiting a higher unemployment before the 1920 Act, reflects a lower unemployment for most of the period since insurance was extended from the fluctuating trades to industry in general. In Chart III dates at which Insurance Acts extending the numbers insured came into effect are marked with an X.

[2] Figures revised to eliminate the Irish Free State from December, 1921.

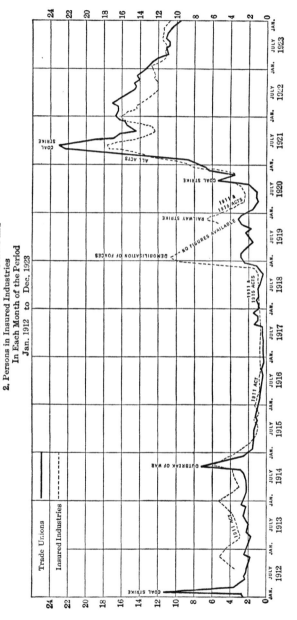

CHART III
PERCENTAGE OF UNEMPLOYMENT
Among
1. Members of Certain Trade Unions and
2. Persons in Insured Industries
In Each Month of the Period
Jan. 1912 to Dec. 1923

Trade Unions
Insured Industries

TABLE XIII — (*Continued*). PERCENTAGES OF UNEMPLOYMENT

| Month (End of) | Trade-Union Percentage | Insured-Trades Percentage |
|---|---|---|
| **1921** | | |
| April | 17.6 | 15.0 |
| May | 22.2 | 17.3 |
| June | 23.1 | 17.8 |
| July | 16.7 | 14.8 |
| August | 16.3 | 13.15 |
| September | 14.8 | 12.2 |
| October | 15.6 | 12.8 |
| November | 15.9 | 15.7 |
| December | 16.5 | 16.1 |
| **1922** | | |
| January | 16.8 | 16.0 |
| February | 16.3 | 15.5 |
| March | 16.3 | 14.4 |
| April | 17.0 | 14.4 |
| May | 16.4 | 13.5 |
| June | 15.7 | 12.7 |
| July | 14.6 | 12.3 |
| August | 14.4 | 12.0 |
| September | 14.6 | 12.0 |
| October | 14.0 | 12.0 |
| November | 14.2 | 12.4 |
| December | 14.0 | 12.6 |
| **1923** | | |
| January | 13.7 | 13.1 |
| February | 13.1 | 12.2 |
| March | 12.3 | 11.5 |
| April | 11.3 | 11.4 |
| May | 11.3 | 11.2 |
| June | 11.1 | 11.3 |
| July | 11.1 | 11.5 |
| August | 11.4 | 11.8 |
| September | 11.3 | 11.7 |
| October | 10.9 | 11.7 |
| November | 10.5 | 11.5 |
| December | 9.7 | 10.7 |
| **1924** | | |
| January | 8.9 | †11.9 |
| February | 8.1 | 10.7 |
| March | 7.8 | 9.9 |
| April | 7.5 | 9.7 |
| May | 7.0 | 9.5 |

For three major reasons, aside from the occasional unreliability of the insured-trades statistics which has

† Undue rise resulting from effects of a railway strike in this month.

been mentioned, the trade-union percentages of unemployment have in this book, except for special purposes, been preferred to those given by the Employment Exchanges. These reasons are:

(1) The insured-trades percentages are comprehensive only since 1920. While figures of unemployment in insured trades go back, of course, to the beginning of national unemployment insurance operation in 1912, they cover only about 2,250,000 workers from 1912 to 1916; 4,000,000 from 1916 to 1920; and the approximately 12,000,000 now insured only since the inauguration of the Act of 1920. These sweeping changes in the numbers on which the percentage of insured-trades unemployment is based makes their use for comparison with the pre-depression period less reliable than is the case with the more consistent trade-union figures.

(2) Although the trade-union statistics were sometimes unduly high as a measure of whole-time unemployment, the insured-trades statistics were as often unduly low as a measure of the real sum of unemployment. They do not take into account short-time, whether or not arranged so as to give the underemployed worker title to benefit. The separate Employment Exchange figures of short-time organized in insured trades so as to permit benefit, published monthly in the Ministry of Labor *Gazette*, cover so small a proportion of total short-time as to make their inclusion with the statistics of complete unemployment undesirable. While underemployment has without question been very great during the depression period, its extent has been so indeterminable that, with reluctance, little attention has been given to it in this study.[1] But there can be no doubt that had it been possi-

[1] An admittedly "very rough estimate" of the extent of underemployment in September, 1922, has been made by the authors of *The Third Winter of Unemployment*, p. 30. Statistics of the number of short-time workers claiming benefit in each month from December, 1920 (410,000) to June, 1923 (60,000) may be found in the *Report on National Unemployment Insurance to July, 1923*, p. 58.

ble to add the partial unemployment due to all short-time
to the complete unemployment in the insured trades, the
resultant percentage of inactive labor would have corre-
sponded more closely to the trade-union than to the insured-trades figures, when the depression was at its worst.

(3) Until May, 1921, there was no closely accurate
estimate of the number of work-people in insured trades,
the Ministry of Labor contenting itself for some months
after passage of the Act of 1920 with an estimate of "about
12,000,000," on which base the insured-trades percentage of unemployment was calculated. In May, 1921,
the first careful compilation of the number of insured
was made, since when the total has been periodically
revised as follows:

| | |
|---|---|
| May, 1921 | 12,190,790 |
| November, 1921 | 11,902,000 |
| March, 1922 | 12,120,000 |
| April, 1922 | 11,880,650 |
| October, 1922 | 11,750,450 |
| July, 1923 | 11,502,800 |

The revision in April, 1922, was due to the contemporary
transference of the administration of unemployment insurance in Southern Ireland to the Government of the
Irish Free State. On January 1, 1922, the Minister of
Labor for Northern Ireland took over its administration
within that area.[1] These changes necessarily for the time
being disorganized Employment Exchange statistics. Since
1922, on the basis of a fundamental revision at the beginning of each insurance year, when Unemployment Books
must be exchanged, and with other revisions based on new
issues of these books to those entering insured trades, the
percentage of complete unemployment in the insured
trades has closely approached accuracy. But for the
various reasons which have been cited the trade-union
percentages of unemployment are obviously preferable

[1] Reciprocal arrangements, under which qualification for benefit
acquired and amount of benefit received in one country are taken
into account in the other, are in operation between Great Britain
and both Irish Governments.

for the years 1921 and 1922 as a whole, in addition to the advantage which they have of being part of a continuous and reasonably uniform record covering a period of over half a century.

## SCOPE OF TRADE-UNION STATISTICS

The trade-union percentages of unemployment are based on returns furnished to the Ministry of Labor by various trade unions which pay unemployment benefit to their members. These returns, compiled monthly, give for each union concerned both the total membership and the total of unemployed at the end of the month, exclusive of members on strike, locked-out, sick, or superannuated. The sum of the latter figures is the numerator, the sum of the former is the denominator, of the fraction which gives the trade-union percentage of unemployment as published monthly in the official Ministry of Labor *Gazette*.

These trade-union returns are very limited in scope, having reference to less than 1,500,000 workers in the following trades: Building; Coal-Mining; Engineering and Shipbuilding; Miscellaneous Metal; Cotton, Woolen and Worsted, and other Textiles; Printing, Bookbinding and Paper; Furnishing and Woodworking; Clothing; Boot and Shoe; Leather; Glass; Pottery; Tobacco. The returns are confined almost entirely to the skilled workers in these trades and do not reflect short-time.

As a quantitative measure of unemployment, even in the specific occupations for which they report, the trade-union returns are of no value. They do not, in the words of Sir William Beveridge, give a "fair sample" of the industrial population.[1] This is well brought out by the following table, comparing the trade-union and insured-trades statistics of unemployment in certain occupations at the end of February, 1923.

[1] See Beveridge: *Unemployment*, pp. 20–23, for a careful analysis of the value of the trade-union statistics on unemployment. The numbers which they cover vary as trade-union membership varies. In May, 1924, membership in the unions reporting had fallen to 1,092,603.

TABLE XIV. COMPARISON OF TRADE-UNION AND INSURED-TRADES STATISTICS

| INDUSTRY | TOTAL NUMBER ON WHICH UNEMPLOYMENT PERCENTAGE IS BASED [1] | | REGISTERED UNEMPLOYMENT AT END OF MONTH [2] | PERCENTAGE OF UNEMPLOYMENT |
|---|---|---|---|---|
| Coal | Trade Union | 134,343 | 8,133 | 6.1 |
| mining | Insured Trade | 1,224,660 | 50,383 | 4.1 |
| Building | Trade Union | 125,226 | 11,102 | 8.9 |
| | Insured Trade | 768,790 | 141,803 | 18.4 |
| Cotton | Trade Union | 60,771 | 4,625 | 7.6 |
| trade | Insured Trade | 601,470 | 63,504 | 10.6 |
| Tobacco | Trade Union | 4,878 | 1,559 | 32.0 |
| manufr. | Insured Trade | 46,960 | 4,023 | 8.6 |
| Boot and | Trade Union | 75,204 | 3,858 | 5.1 |
| shoe trade | Insured Trade | 150,380 | 12,323 | 8.2 |

The above table throws into relief the inadequacy of the trade-union statistics for giving any indication of the volume of unemployment as a whole. Aside from the fact that they do not touch several important industries, such as transport services, it is obvious that the trade-union returns do not correctly reflect conditions in the trades which they do represent. This is shown to exaggeration by the figures given in Table XIV for tobacco manufacture. The trade-union returns in this trade are supplied by unions whose members are mainly cigarmakers, among whom unemployment was very widespread during the depression. But for tobacco, cigar and cigarette manufacture as a whole the percentage of unemployment at the end of February, 1923, was only about one quarter as high. The trade-union figures for the building trade, on the

[1] In the case of the trade-union figures, this number is the membership at the end of February, 1923, of the union reporting. In the case of the insured-trades figure, it is the Ministry of Labor estimate, based on Unemployment Books issued, of the total number in each trade.

[2] The insured-trades figure is the number of Unemployment Books remaining lodged February 26, 1923.

other hand, relating for the most part to carpenters and plumbers, show unemployment of under nine per cent. But when the total includes bricklayers, plasterers, painters, laborers, and others who are equally members of this industry, the percentage of unemployment is seen to be double.

The trade-union returns, to sum up, give no reliable information as to the volume of unemployment, either in the whole of industry or in any particular industry. For a measure of volume the insured-trades statistics have therefore been utilized in this study, although subject to defects which have been noted. It is worth observing at this point that by adopting the seemingly simple expedient of refusing to let an insured worker withdraw his Unemployment Book until evidence of his employment had been furnished the Exchange, a really reliable figure of the total volume of unemployment at all periods could be attained.

Nevertheless, the trade-union statistics, incomplete as they are, provide a very fair index of the degree of unemployment in Great Britain at any time during the past fifty years. They are the best source available as to the general trend of unemployment and are also, within their recognized limits, surprisingly accurate. The motives tending to make a skilled trade unionist stay on his union register after exhausting right to benefit are stronger than the motives which urge the ordinary worker in similar case to leave his Unemployment Book at the Exchange. There is a feeling of loyalty towards the union, absent in his attitude towards the Exchange. There is the union rule that if unemployed he must sign the union Vacant Book, whether or not in receipt of benefit, which is customarily strengthened by the provision that if registered as unemployed he is excused from payment of contributions; and finally there is the fact that employers or their foremen will often notify a vacancy to the local of the skilled trade union when the Exchange would be overlooked. These facts help to explain why the trade-union statistics, although so limited in scope, have proved a surprisingly good index of the extent of unemployment for many years. Unreliable as a measure of total unemployment they nevertheless furnish a very reliable indication of the general trend of unemployment. Whatever their percentage of error, it is a constant one from month to month and year to year.

GENERAL STATISTICAL WORK OF THE EXCHANGES

The criticism implied in the foregoing is that the Employment Exchanges, in spite of the labor expended on statistical work, have failed to furnish useful information regarding unemployment in Great Britain. Such criticism without due qualification would be most unjust.

In the first place, evidence that neither the Live Register figures nor the number of Vacant Books lodged has in the past been exhaustive of the total number unemployed is no derogation of the general statistical work of the Exchanges. Inadequacy in one respect has been stressed at length. Let that emphasis set off the fact that in all respects where the necessary limitations are understood their statistical work is remarkably accurate. Occasionally figures which seem superfluous may be collected, and in some respects the Exchanges furnish returns which do inadequate justice to their own work.[1] But on definite problems and within their definite scope it is beyond question that the Exchange statistics may be relied on.

In the second place, while the Exchanges have not yet been able to give the total of unemployment at any moment with positive accuracy, the light which they can cast on its extent constitutes tremendous advance in view of the complete absence of statistics on the quantity of unemployment in Great Britain even a decade ago, and in view of the meager statistical information available in the United

[1] As in the fact that general statistics of vacancies filled do not include placings of casual labor, and that thousands of placings are made through the indirect instrumentality of the Exchanges which are not recorded at all. Cf. Cmd. 1140 (1921), p. 65.

States and other highly industrialized nations to-day.[1] So far as the insured trades go, covering approximately twelve million workers and every important body of wage-earners except agriculturalists and domestic servants, the machinery of unemployment registration in Great Britain is now complete. All those falling out of employment — excepting the almost negligible fraction who do not mind losing their claim to benefit — are almost automatically registered as unemployed. That some go off the records while remaining workless is no fault of the Exchange statistical service. And this deficiency could be remedied by making it compulsory for the unemployed worker to keep his Vacant Book lodged during the whole period of unemployment.

Finally, it should be noted that the supposititious value of knowing the total of unemployment in the country at any given moment is to a large extent fictitious. Even if the total were accurately determinable, it is difficult to see how solution of the problem of unemployment would be at all advanced thereby. The knowledge would be of small assistance in distinguishing out the relative importance of the factors involved; whether temporary or permanent; personal or impersonal; avertible or unavoidable; commercial, financial, or industrial; seasonal or cyclical; national or international.

What is desirable, and highly desirable, for any scientific treatment of unemployment is that there should be available reliable information, *first*, as to whether the whole volume of unemployment is increasing, diminishing, or stationary from one week, month, or year to another; and, *second*, as to the alteration of conditions of employment in each important industry. For the first of these purposes the trade-union statistics have, in the past, served better than those furnished by the Exchanges. For the second, the Exchange statistics, covering a very wide field and

---

[1] Cf. *Special Report on the Unemployment Enquiry of the International Labor Office, 1922*, pp. 10–18 and p. 21.

including unskilled as well as skilled labor, are the only reliable source of information at the present time.

It would be unfair, in short, to judge the future statistical work of the Exchanges by their past shortcomings alone. Their statistical work is steadily improving in value, and any development of the program of unemployment relief which would interfere without supplying some equally potential source of information in its place, should be discouraged. This, among other reasons to be discussed in the next chapter, makes it advisable that industries which establish their own systems of unemployment insurance should continue to utilize the Employment Exchanges as placing agencies.

# CHAPTER XI

## THE LESSON FOR THE FUTURE

FREE Public Employment Exchanges in Great Britain date back to the Unemployed Workmen Act of 1905. As a national system the experiment has been tested by practical experience since the Labor Exchanges Act came into operation on February 1, 1910. That experience, long enough to allow a reasoned judgment to be passed, shows that in periods of trade activity and periods of trade depression alike, the Exchanges have rendered excellent service in bringing unemployed workers and vacant jobs together quickly and efficiently. They have improved the mobility of labor. They have probably done something towards maintaining the level of purchasing power — and thereby stabilizing trade — by cutting down the loss of time to both employer and wage-earner involved in labor transferences. They have been able to render useful statistical information on the quantity, extent, incidence, and alteration of unemployment, information which is essential for any rational program of unemployment relief. Although their value as placing agencies has been questionable for some of the highly skilled, thoroughly organized trades, there can be no doubt of the immense service they have rendered for the poorly organized trades and for seasonal workers. Except indirectly and to an almost negligible extent, the Exchanges have done nothing to solve the fundamental problem of regularizing the demand for labor. That is not surprising. It is not in their nature to be able to do anything important in this direction.

The Employment Exchanges, in a sentence, have proved themselves able to provide the requisite information and the requisite machinery for a scientific program of lessening the duration and some of the ill-effects of individual unemployment. So well-grounded and acceptable have they become in the eyes of the nation as a whole, that it was possible through their agency in 1920 to make the registration of unemployment practically compulsory for the great majority of the wage-earning population.

Yet the fact remains that the Exchanges are at present so hampered in their operation that few of their potential benefits can be realized. It is, for instance, impossible under present conditions to make the notification of vacancies compulsory. For an effective organization of the "Labor Market" and to cut the vicious circle in which Employment Exchange operation is now bound, this compulsory notification — which need not mean compulsory utilization — will probably have to be brought about.[1] But this and other needed improvements cannot be instituted until the burden of State-operated unemployment insurance on the Exchanges has been lessened.

### THE STRAIN OF STATE–OPERATED INSURANCE

Once State-operated unemployment insurance was initiated (and the first Unemployment Insurance Act was passed by Parliament only twenty-seven months after the Labor Exchanges Act), the Employment Exchanges never had a fair chance. They were barely launched before the operation of unemployment insurance was grafted upon them. Two years after this, when the additional duties of insurance had scarcely been learned, the Exchanges were plunged into abnormal war activities. Immediately after the Armistice came out-of-work donations, followed by the Unemployment Insurance Act of 1920. Before the tremendous expansion of work involved in this Act had been mastered the depression period set in, with new Unemployment Insurance Acts following one another at intervals of a few months. The thoughts and energy of those who should have had as their first duty improvement in the placing work of the Exchanges were absorbed in keeping up

[1] See pp. 112-13.

with the endless detail of a protean insurance program. The effect of these Acts in hampering the development of placing work can scarcely be exaggerated. Truly, it is not surprising that so few of the potential benefits of the Employment Exchanges have been realized. On the contrary, it is little short of remarkable that in spite of the terrific burden of unemployment insurance they have held their own so well.

A main reason for loading the operation of insurance on the Exchanges was that they provided a means of testing unemployment. A great deal of effort, which might have gone into the development of placing work, has been expended by the Exchanges in trying to insure effective checks against fraud. Yet so dubious have been the results that benefits have had to be kept at a level in itself sufficiently low to prevent malingering. Because of this it has been impossible to prevent the practise of double relief — unemployment insurance benefit and Poor Relief — which in turn has encouraged fraud. Again, the fact that employers are not bound to notify their vacancies to the Exchanges permits a leakage in the Unemployment Fund. "The leakage may not be so serious in the case of trade-union applicants," observes the report of the Committee of Enquiry on Employment Exchanges held in 1920, "since the employer may be in touch with the union, but in respect of workers in unorganized industries the fund is not equally safeguarded against malingering or delay."[1] Here is a broad hint that there would be likely to be less, rather than more, fraud, the more unemployment insurance were dissociated from the Exchanges and attached to well-organized industries. While the amount of fraudulent claiming during the depression period is easily exaggerated, it has been by no means inconsiderable. From the Armistice to July, 1923, there were upwards of 5400 prosecutions for improper claims that had been detected, as compared with under 150 prosecutions in the first six years of insurance.

[1] Cmd. 1054 (1920), p. 13.

INSURANCE IN NAME ONLY

Since the war State-operated unemployment insurance has, under any strict interpretation of the word "insurance," been little more than a name. Outright doles in the shape of Out-of-Work Donation practically supplanted insurance for a year after the Armistice, and to a lesser degree continued well into 1921. When there were still almost 356,000 individuals drawing Out-of-Work Donation, the Act of March, 1921, first of the degeneration Unemployment Insurance Acts, came into operation.[1] Outright doles in the shape of Out-of-Work Donation and disguised doles in the shape of "uncovenanted benefit" actually overlapped.

Nor is it possible to find any advantage in the fact that the State allowance continued to be called "insurance" during the depression period. The enormous increase in Employment Exchange staffs necessary to operate unemployment insurance without any improvement in the extent of placing work has been pointed out.[2] It has been shown that under the Act of March, 1923, over ninety-eight per cent of the uncovenanted benefit allowed adult male workers ineligible for dependants' grants could have been paid as an outright dole for the allotted benefit period without additional cost.[3] When there is taken into consideration the saving in time, energy, and personnel which a dole system would have permitted, it is obvious that this alternative would have been much cheaper. It is to be remembered that by the Act of March, 1923, uncovenanted benefit at the rate of forty-six weeks in fifty-two was allowed when "expedient in the public interest,"[4] without reference to contributions and with practically no conditions except willingness to work, and that the Exchanges

[1] Cf. p. 31.
[2] See pp. 120–22.
[3] See Table VIII, p. 95.
[4] See Sub-section (1) of Section 4 of the Act of April, 1922, and Sub-section (3) of Section 1 of the Act of March, 1923.

were not in a position thoroughly to ensure even this one proviso. These things considered, it is impossible to see in what way, except in additional expense, effort, and complications, State-operated unemployment insurance in its degeneration differed from, or was preferable to, a regulated system of doles, with all the obvious defects of such a system.

To assert that no system of unemployment insurance could have withstood the post-war depression in Great Britain is to burke the issue with an argument the validity of which is questionable. The point is that State-operated unemployment insurance did not "make good." In Chapter VI it was shown that the State system was not only inadequately prepared for a test which should have been anticipated, but that it went to pieces with a rapidity indicating it would have been insufficient defence for a depression of normal duration and extent. It is perfectly true, but at best only an excuse, to say that the failure to extend insurance until the onset of the depression hastened collapse. And this excuse is in itself a very serious indictment of the ability of the State to handle the problem with adequate intelligence and foresight. Not the device of unemployment insurance, but that device under State management has been found wanting.

OTHER DEFECTS OF THE STATE INSURANCE SYSTEM

Aside from the manner in which it has hampered Employment Exchange operation, State-operated unemployment insurance, during its decline period, exhibited other serious defects. In spite of the complications introduced it completely failed to provide an adequate scheme of relief. The national system had to be supported by Poor Law relief in every part of the country; the result of this double system being not only to encourage fraud, but also to increase local taxation in the very districts where its easing was probably most necessary for trade recovery. Similarly restrictive was the abnormality of having the scale of contributions from employers and employed high when trade was bad and low when trade was good. During the depression period the State insurance system, as will be seen by reference to the tables in Chapter V, steadily increased the financial penalty on employers. Just prior to the depression the employer paid a weekly insurance contribution of four pence in respect of each adult male worker employed. By April, 1922, this weekly per capita contribution had been raised to ten pence. By strange inverted logic the employer was made to pay most heavily for giving employment when unemployment was worst.

### FUNCTIONS OF STATE AND INDUSTRY

The British effort to weld together Employment Exchange operation and that of State-operated unemployment insurance has proved a failure. It has been so not because of any intrinsic demerit in either device for relieving unemployment. Nor has it failed by reason of shortcomings on the part of Government employees, whose steadfast devotion to onerous duties has greatly mitigated what would otherwise have been a much more obvious collapse. At bottom, failure has been due to a lack of appreciation of the proper function of the State in relation to unemployment relief.

That the State is the necessary agency for handling Employment Exchange operation effectively is obvious. The problem here is the organization of the "Labor Market," a problem external to any particular industry, something beyond the power of any industry to solve for itself. There should be a large amount of specialization in the Employment Exchange system. In every important city certain Exchanges should cater exclusively to certain predominant industries. But State control of the system as a whole is necessary, not only for the sake of poorly organized industries; not only to integrate industry as a whole; but also because the Exchanges are the basis of all satisfactory schemes for the provision of work, and because they provide machinery on which unemployment insurance, even when dissociated from State operation, will for a long time depend.

There remains the question as to where should rest responsibility for the relief of that unemployment which will continue, however effective the State mechanism for bringing jobless worker and workless job together. Is this also a function of the State? To some extent, but only in a collaborative sense.

The actual provision of employment, whether through long-range planning of public works, export credit schemes, or measures akin to the Trade Facilities Act,[1] will probably become increasingly a duty of the State during periods of depression. The actual relief of existing unemployment, on the other hand, should be handled by the State only in so far as it cannot be handled effectively and economically by industry itself. A part — a large part — of insurance against unemployment must in all probability remain under State operation in Great Britain for years to come. This does not alter the fact that unemployment insurance should, at least in normal times, be handled by industry itself, if necessary with State subventions roughly proportionate to the extent that unemployment is not an internal problem of industry itself.

That the change of policy involved will result in a very considerable reduction in the rate of unemployment is not argued. That there are numerous formidable obstacles in the way of inaugurating even a partial scheme of insurance by industry is not for a moment disputed. But that the change would give industry both the incentive and the opportunity to attempt constructive solution, so far as within its power lies, of one of the most urgent of industrial problems is unquestionable.

[1] An adequate analysis of the British Export Credits Scheme and Trade Facilities Act is found in *The Third Winter of Unemployment*, pp. 54-57. These, and other emergency measures for the provision of employment in Great Britain during the depression period, are summarized in Appendix VI.

The principle at stake is in strict accord with the dominant political philosophy of the times. On no other current industrial question is there such unanimity of opinion, among employers, labor spokesmen, and independent economists, as on the thesis that the furtherance of industrial self-government is the course pointed by circumstance as advisable. Trust magnates and Guild Socialists are on common ground in upholding the responsibility of industry for managing its own problems. So far as this is compatible with public interest, and there is no inherent reason why it should not be, the non-industrial classes are in hearty accord with this theory. In steadily increasing degree since the war, the tendency has been for a better regularization of industry by industry. In every western nation the different industries have begun to take on corporate form. There has been great improvement in employers' organization; in labor organization; in the machinery of coöperation between the two through such agencies as Joint Industrial Councils. And against this almost universal concentration on furtherance of vocational responsibility, the development of standardized unemployment insurance as a function of the bureaucratic State stands out in sharp and questionable contrast.

Various recent British Administrations have shown that they appreciate the value of the movement towards insurance by industry. Under the Lloyd George régime this was affirmed by the Minister of Labor in a letter addressed to practically all organizations of employers and employed in Great Britain on February 22, 1922. The policy of the Government has been, the Minister wrote, "to do everything possible to encourage industries to administer their own schemes for dealing with those of their work-people who become unemployed . . . and as soon as the state of the Unemployment Fund permits I shall again welcome and encourage the establishment of special schemes for dealing with unemployment insurance on an industrial basis." In more cautious terms this policy received the general endorsement of the Ministry of Labor under the Bonar Law and Baldwin Governments. The Labor Party, however, for reasons which are apparently based on fear that employers may gain too preponderant an influence in the control of unemployment insurance, has exhibited a tendency actively to oppose the trend towards insurance by industry. Legislation introduced in the House of Commons with the endorsement of this party on April 3, 1924, contained a clause designed to abolish the power to establish special schemes of insurance by industry even after the close of the deficiency period. Though modified by a provision authorizing the continuance of any special scheme either approved or submitted in complete form before April 3, 1924, this endeavor to close an avenue of escape from the stereotyped State-operated system must, on the whole, be regarded as most unfortunate. It indicates a failure on the part of the Labor Party executives to recognize the fundamental defects in the national scheme as brought out by the depression period; a failure the more striking because of the strong opposition to bureaucratic methods frequently voiced by many of Labor's most able spokesmen.[1]

### Dissociation from State Operation

It is not the purpose of this study to examine the most complicated problem of insurance by industry in close detail. It has been the writer's purpose to show that the present State-operated system is played out and that concentration on insurance by industry has become necessary, assuming that it is desirable to maintain unemployment insurance and not attempt to shelve the problem by the inglorious and demoralizing device of doles. In broad outline, however, the method which should be fol-

---

[1] But it was the Labor Party which inaugurated the special scheme of unemployment insurance for the banking industry after its predecessors had deferred approval. Cf. p. 46, footnote.

lowed in dissociating unemployment insurance from State operation can be pointed out. But at the outset it is necessary to emphasize that no such form of company-controlled unemployment insurance as is being worked by the National Federation of Employees' Approved Societies (see p. 41) is necessarily endorsed. Except as it can be regarded as a step towards real insurance by industry — as opposed to paternalistic insurance by individual employers — the "Lesser" scheme is a retrogression rather than an advance. Indeed the movement towards vesting the control of unemployment insurance administration in the hands of employers does much to explain the disappointing, but precautionary, attitude lately taken by the Labor Party with respect to contracting out.

Nevertheless, with this proviso, it is clear that at the earliest possible opportunity a start in the development of insurance by industry should be made by permitting well-organized trades with a relatively low percentage of unemployment to contract out of the present national scheme. There is no necessity for postponing this step for the long time which must elapse until the end of the deficiency period, as was ordered by the Act of July, 1921. The purpose of this ruling was to protect the Unemployment Fund by preventing the withdrawal from the national scheme of insured workers who are "good risks." Should industries with low unemployment withdraw from the national scheme, it was argued, the burden of raising benefits for the "poor risks" which do not contract out will be intolerable during the depression period.

Since industries with relatively low unemployment are under the national scheme paying for the high unemployment in other industries, it should not be difficult to make arrangements whereby they would still "spread the risk," in accordance with the general principle of insurance, while contracting out of the State-operated system. Among suggestions which have been put forward towards this end, that of the Joint Industrial Council of

the Wallpaper Industry has the cardinal merit of sim-
plicity. It provides that when a well-organized trade
with a low percentage of unemployment contracts out
of the national scheme, half of the reduction of contribution and half of the increase of benefit which the low
unemployment in this trade permits should be handed
over to the State-operated Unemployment Fund. The
idea is outlined as follows by Mr. A. V. Sugden, Chairman of Executive of the Wallpaper Manufacturers,
Ltd., in the *Manchester Guardian Commercial* of February 8, 1923:

> If the national contribution were fixed at 1s. per week and
> the benefit rate 20s., and an organized trade found it could work
> the necessary scheme at 10d. per week levy and at 25s. benefit,
> then that society would charge its members 11d. per week, and
> grant 22s. 6d. benefit, handing over 1d. per week of its income
> from each member and 2s. 6d. per week of each 25s. of benefit
> granted to the National Scheme Fund.

Once satisfactory arrangements of this general nature
have been agreed upon between Joint Industrial Councils
of well-organized industries on the one hand and the
Ministry of Labor on the other, the approval of the Government Actuary being understood, it only remains for
the industries contracting out to set up and operate their
special schemes, individually adapted to the requirements
of the particular industry. In practically all cases, however, the industry would notify its vacancies to the National Employment Exchange system and rely on the
Exchanges, though not necessarily to the detriment of
additional measures, for the filling of vacant jobs.[1] Between
the insurance organization of the industry and the Exchanges there should be the closest coöperation, furthering

[1] In the Insurance Industry the attempt of dispensing with the
Employment Exchanges has been made. Although this industry is
exceptional, most of its employees being clerical workers, it is dubious
that the policy attempted has proved wise. Normally, at least, no
attempt should be made to dispense with the assistance of the Employment Exchanges.

that reasonable uniformity in the different schemes which is desirable, helping to check labor "poaching" in times of good employment and selfish exclusiveness in times of bad employment.

Responsibility for giving the unemployed worker every facility to find employment as quickly as possible would thus be a function of the State. Financial responsibility for its unemployed would be as far as possible a function of each particular industry. And State subventions to such industrial insurance funds as can prove the need of assistance should be designed in such a way as to encourage rather than lessen industrial responsibility. A point of great importance for every industry establishing a special scheme to observe is the advisability of making the employer pay contributions in respect of *unemployment*, instead of in respect of *employment* as is the case under State-operated insurance.

### SOME OBJECTIONS ANSWERED

Reasonably reliable statistics on the incidence of unemployment in the different British industries are now available. For those industries that are well organized, corporate in form, and relatively active all the year round, a cautious but immediate start in insurance by industry seems entirely possible, provided, as is coming to be more and more the case, that there is the will on the part of both employers and employed to contract out of the national scheme. The objection often raised, that the result would be to drive a further wedge between the aristocracy of highly skilled workers and the mass of the unskilled, is not well founded. It is based on the fallacious assumption that insurance by *industry* would be insurance by *trade* in the narrow sense of the word. But one great virtue of the project is that the industry contracting out would insure the unskilled as well as the skilled workers connected with it. For the unorganized, unattached wage-earner a nucleus of the present national scheme will long remain. There would be the constant incentive for all workers of this type to attach themselves permanently to some stable industry. Insurance by industry would encourage labor unionism on broad industrial lines just as it would encourage more complete organization by employers within an industry.

There are other, more cogent, objections. The reader may judge for himself whether those of them which appear to be important are in reality of an unsurmountable nature.

(1) Industries are not clearly marked off one from another, and the demarcation between them necessary for contracting out of the national scheme is undoubtedly a very difficult problem. Nevertheless, as was pointed out on page 24, it was found possible to achieve a quite workable demarcation of insured from uninsured trades in the early days of the national system, and there is no reason to suppose the task inherently more difficult for industries now than it was for such "trades" as building, shipbuilding, and engineering in 1913. It would, of course, be eminently desirable to retain the umpire (a Crown official) as final arbiter in demarcation disputes.

(2) Seasonal and casual employments, which cause many wage-earners (particularly the unskilled) to work for several different industries in the course of a year, provide a problem somewhat akin to demarcation. But it is questionable whether this problem is as serious as it appears. Such laborers, who after all are a small proportion of the whole industrial population, might well receive benefit from the industry to which they were attached when becoming unemployed through no fault of their own. This policy would have the distinct advantage of discouraging casual employment. And, excepting in such occupations as agriculture, it would add force to the natural pressure on "seasonal employers" to turn their attention to kindred but more stable lines of manufacture in off-season periods.

(3) Accurate knowledge of the rate of unemployment in each industry contracting out is required for establishing successful rates of contribution and benefit in its industrial insurance scheme. Through the Employment Exchange statistics, however, the incidence of unemployment in different industries is now fairly accurately known. That which is most important in this connection — the extent of unemployment in different occupations at the height of a most serious depression — has been reliably ascertained. In most major industries actuarial computation could readily establish rates having every prospect of maintaining the various Unemployment Funds solvent throughout the trade cycle. They would be much less experimental than the rates of contribution and benefit for the national scheme have been.

(4) Too much compulsion might be involved in the administration of insurance by industry. It is difficult to see how there would be any more compulsion than under the existing system, and the probability is there would be much less. Moreover, the indication is that objections of this nature are not directed against compulsion and discipline exerted within a democratically organized and controlled industry, but against compulsion exercised through the external agency of the State. Ample evidence of the possibility of self-discipline where the corporate spirit in industry exists is found in the work of the Joint Industrial Councils.[1] Testimony of representative employers and trade unionists, before the Government Committee of Enquiry on Employment Exchanges, which sat in 1920, coincided in the view that the form rather than the fact of compulsion has been the detriment in State-operated unemployment insurance.

(5) Under the 1920 Act schemes for insurance by industry must in general be formulated with the approval of a Joint Industrial Council or other joint association of

[1] Cf. the official *Report on the Establishment and Progress of Joint Industrial Councils*, 1917–22.

employers and employed sufficiently representative to carry the assent of an unquestioned majority of those concerned. The question arises whether industry has as yet reached the stage of coöperative organization where special schemes, difficult enough to work out under favorable circumstances, can be drawn so as to reconcile the various interests within an industry.

To this question there is a twofold answer. In the first place the energy with which the study of insurance by industry was taken up by Joint Industrial Councils, prior to the abrogation in June, 1921, of the right of contracting out, indicates a will of the nature which in time generally finds a practical way.[1] And this will has been greatly strengthened by the depression period collapse of the State-operated system. In the second place this problem naturally solves itself. For except where industry shows the desire and the ability to present plans of unemployment insurance with a fair prospect of success, there is no chance of insurance by industry being introduced, even when the present legal ban on the adoption of special schemes is removed.

## INSURANCE BY INDUSTRY IN OPERATION

In concluding this survey it will be advantageous to examine the only special scheme which has been put into actual operation in Great Britain — that for the Insurance Industry. As pointed out in Chapter IV, this industry is in several respects peculiar, and the success with which its special scheme has met cannot be taken as a fair index of what might be expected when more representative industries contract out of the national system.[2] Certain economies and simplifications which it has introduced, however, would seem equally possible wherever unemployment insurance is placed on an industrial basis.

The Insurance Industry Unemployment Insurance Scheme came into operation on July 4, 1921, and covers

[1] See p. 44.         [2] See p. 47.

approximately 85,000 insured persons, of which number, roughly speaking, 57,000 are males and 28,000 females. From the financial viewpoint the Scheme has been eminently successful, in spite of the facts that employees pay no contributions, and that benefits have been twenty-five per cent higher than those established for the national system in July, 1921. The balance sheet for the first year's working was as follows:

TABLE XV. FIRST ANNUAL BALANCE SHEET, INSURANCE
INDUSTRY SPECIAL SCHEME

| | | |
|---|---:|---:|
| Contributions under Scheme | £153,978 | |
| Sum due from State Unemployment Fund (under Act of 1920, Section 18, par. 10)[1] for period November 8, 1920, to July 4, 1921 | 68,000 | |
| State Grant (under Act of 1920, Section 18, par. 7)[1] | 8,800 | |
| | £230,778 | |
| Profit on investments realized | 1,803 | |
| Interest received and accrued | 3,801 | |
| | | £236,382 |
| Expenditure on benefit | £31,651 | |
| Expenditure on administration | 17,672 | 49,323 |
| Surplus on July 1, 1922 | | £187,059 |

The above figures show that the Insurance Industry could have dispensed with all State subventions, paid into the National Unemployment Fund as its share in "spreading the risk" of unemployment a sum equal to one half of contributions paid in plus one half of benefits paid out (a hypothetical arrangement a great deal more generous than that outlined on page 154), and still have had a surplus of between £10,000 and £15,000 at the end of the first year's operation of its Special Scheme. The inference is that the Ministry of Labor may have forwarded, rather than checked, the insolvency of the State Unemployment Fund by prohibiting other industries with low employment from contracting out during the depression period. It should be noted that the ratio of administrative expenses

[1] Cf. Appendix II, p. 175.

to income — 5.5 per cent — is much lower than the best record ever achieved by the national system.

Aside from the very low rate of unemployment in the Insurance Industry, this excellent financial record is undoubtedly partly due to the fact that three out of the six persons responsible for the scheme were professional actuaries.[1] Actuarial advice, indeed, may be regarded as the first essential in formulating any successful scheme of insurance by industry.

Subject to certain exceptions the scheme applies to all persons insurable under the National Insurance Acts who are in the service of:

(a) Undertakings engaged in the United Kingdom in the granting of insurances under contract.[2]

(b) Undertakings in the United Kingdom engaged in the administration of any system of insurance established by Act of Parliament. This covers approved societies and trade unions so far as they have staff exclusively engaged on national health or unemployment insurance work.

The exceptions are:

(1) Persons engaged as housekeepers, or in cleaning and maintenance or other manual labor, unless such persons are in the exclusive employment of an insurance undertaking and are employed for the purposes of such undertaking.

(2) Employees of persons or companies combining insurance undertakings with other undertakings, unless the employment is exclusively in connection with the insurance undertaking.

(3) Employees in the service of the Crown or of the Insurance Committees established under the National Health Insurance Acts.

[1] See an anonymous article by one of the committee which drafted the Insurance Industry Special Scheme, in the *Manchester Guardian Commercial* of December 14, 1922.

[2] This Special Scheme applies to Ireland, subject in the case of the Irish Free State to certain local adjustments, in the same way as to Great Britain.

In case of doubt, the question whether any person or class of persons falls within the Scheme is decided by the Minister of Labor, subject to an appeal to a single judge of the High Court, whose decision is final. It is noteworthy that questions of demarcation have not been numerous, partly because of the compact and highly organized character of the Insurance Industry.

### ADMINISTRATION OF THE INSURANCE INDUSTRY SCHEME

The Scheme is administered by a Joint Board of ten persons comprising five representatives of employers and five of employees. Its original members were nominated by the Joint Association of employers and employees which promoted the Scheme. Members of the Board hold office normally for two years, retiring in rotation, new members being appointed in accordance with arrangements made by this body.

The insurance fund is established under the control of the Joint Board, into which all receipts are paid and from which all payments are made. Balances may be invested in Trustee Securities. An auditor approved by the Minister of Labor audits the accounts. While the Minister may restrict administrative expenses to a fixed proportion of the income of the fund, it has not been found necessary to do so.

Subject to a general financial supervision not dissimilar to that exercised by the Government over limited liability companies, the administration of the Scheme is, therefore, independent of State control. Instead of the bureaucratic rulings which govern the national system of unemployment insurance, that in force for the insurance industry is democratically controlled by a Board of Management equally representative of employers and employees. In the rates of contribution and benefits, in the arrangements for collecting and paying these, and in other matters of administration, the Insurance Industry Scheme differs notably from the regulations of the Unemployment Insurance Acts.

No contributions are paid by employees, although it is laid down that, if there is a deficiency after the Scheme has been in operation seven years (that is, in 1928), a contribution equal to one half that payable by those insured under the national system may be imposed. The employers' contributions at the close of 1922 were at the rate of ten pence a week in respect of each male employee and eight pence a week in respect of each female employee. There is no separate rate of contribution for juveniles, and therefore no encouragement to employ juveniles rather than adults as is the case under the Unemployment Insurance Acts.

Weekly benefit rates in the Insurance Industry during 1923 were twenty shillings for men, sixteen shillings for women, and half these rates respectively for boys and girls under eighteen years of age. Other things being equal, therefore, employers who must lay off workers are encouraged to begin with juveniles. This, however, is also true of the scale of benefits under the national system. For a dependent wife (or invalided husband) additional benefit of five shillings a week is allowed, and one shilling for each dependent child.[1]

The rates of benefit mentioned at the beginning of the last paragraph are temporary. Normal rates, designed to come into operation at the close of the second insurance year of the Scheme, are seventeen shillings per week for men, fourteen shillings per week for women, and half rates for boys and girls. It is established that the benefit rates for men and women shall be at least two shillings above, and for boys and girls at least one shilling above, the corresponding weekly rates of benefit under the national system. The periods of benefit correspond generally to those in force under the national system.

### SIMPLIFICATIONS INTRODUCED

It is not, however, with reference to rates of contribution and benefit, which must depend primarily on the rate of

[1] Cf. p. 58.

unemployment in the particular industry, that the Insurance Industry Scheme is most instructive. Its real value as an example of how State-operated unemployment insurance can be improved upon is seen in the machinery for the collection of contributions.

This machinery consists of a system of quarterly payments in advance from employers in respect of the number of employed persons on their personnel list each quarter day, the payment being unaffected by changes in the number employed during the quarter. At the beginning of the three-months period "each employer prepares a list of staff coming under the provisions of the Scheme, and thereafter is merely required to notify name, sex, and date, whenever any new employee is accepted or any existing employee leaves. From this it is easy to agree upon each quarter date the number of employees of each category at that moment employed, and the contribution is made of a full quarter's payment for each such employee. Thus, apart from notifying arrivals and departures,[1] there is merely a reference to what one may describe as a perpetual inventory and the writing of a cheque four times a year." [2]

In other words, anything overpaid in respect of insured persons leaving before the three-months period is over, for all practical purposes balances what is underpaid in respect of insured persons taken on after the three-months period has started. The contrast with the weekly payments and the whole arduous process of weekly accounting under State-operated unemployment insurance illustrates the sort of common-sense simplifications which may be expected to result wherever unemployment insurance is taken over from the State by the more practical minds of industry.

[1] In the first year of operation there were about 20,000 of these changes. (Cmd. 1613, of 1923, p. 36.)

[2] The quotation is from the article in the *Manchester Guardian Commercial* referred to on p. 160.

## OTHER REGULATIONS

The remaining features of the Insurance Industry Scheme present no points particularly worthy of imitation, and may be briefly passed over. The conditions and disqualifications for receipt of benefit are practically the same as those laid down by the Act of 1920, although uncovenanted benefit has been allowed under the Scheme during the depression period. Transference from the national to the special scheme, or *vice versa*, has aroused no difficult problems, partly because there are no arrangements for "transfer values."

During the insurance year ended June 30, 1922, there were 4300 claims for benefit under the Scheme, this figure representing five per cent of the number insured. All authorization of claims is made by the principal office, in London. For the most part claims reach this center either direct, through the last employer, or through the Board's local representatives, to whom application may be made in the first instance. Every claim must be accompanied by a certificate issued by the employer when the insured person is discharged, and giving particulars necessary for assessment of the claim by the principal office. When he receives the certificate the discharged person fills out a receipt which is forwarded by the employer to the principal office, together with a brief statement of the circumstances under which employment was terminated. By comparing the signatures and other particulars on the receipt with the application for benefit the principal office satisfies itself that the claimant is the same person to whom the corresponding certificate was issued. If it is clear that the claim is valid it is authorized and referred for payment to a local "paying officer," of whom upwards of two thousand have been appointed.

The paying officer may be the representative of an insurance undertaking in the district where the claim arose, or the representative of an association of employed persons to which the claimant belongs, and which the Joint Board has authorized to pay benefit under the Scheme to unemployed members who are qualified. Such arrangements, of which six had been put in operation at the beginning of 1923, are limited to associations of employed persons in the Insurance Industry. It is a further condition that these employees' associations should themselves provide unemployment benefit for their membership out of their own funds, in addition to the benefit provided under the Scheme.

The benefit recipient is required to attend periodically at the office of his paying officer, in order to sign the unemployed register at prescribed hours. In addition to being available at all times for vacancies which may be notified, he may be required to furnish from time to time information of his own activities, such as answering advertisements and enquiring of employers, in seeking work.

Vacancies in the Insurance Industry are notified to the principal office of the Joint Board. In the London district they are brought to the notice of claimants when they attend at the Central Office to sign the unemployed register. Notice of vacancies elsewhere is relayed out from the Central Office by mail.

It is noteworthy that the power of making notification of vacancies by employers compulsory is held in reserve under the Scheme, though use of this power was not made during its first two years of operation. A difficulty experienced by the Joint Board has been that the vacancies notified have been insufficient in number, in addition to not being of a sufficiently varied character. Many claims under the Scheme relate to persons on the fringe of the industry, such as caretakers, doorkeepers, etc., or work-people who have left other vocations to obtain employment in the Insurance Industry as outside agents. The vacancies notified to the Joint Board, on the other hand, have been mainly of a clerical type. Utilization of the Employment Exchange machinery would help to adjust the difficulties here. The experiment of the Insurance Industry in ignoring the utility of the Employment Exchanges as labor clearing houses, serves to strengthen the view that the Employment Exchange machinery, in its true function, must be built up and not abandoned.

## CONCLUSIONS

To sum up, it may be said that the record of the first scheme of Unemployment Insurance by Industry has, in spite of all shortcomings, demonstrated the possibility, the practicality, and the advisability of devolution. On the one hand there is the fact that the Insurance Industry is exceptional, as, in the final analysis, are all industries. On the other hand there is the fact that as soon as the Insurance Industry was empowered to administer its own scheme of unemployment insurance, notable simplifications and economies were introduced in a way which is apparently beyond the power of State-operated unemployment insurance. While the latter system has become more and more hopelessly involved and degenerate, the one case in which insurance by industry has been tried has proved itself a notable success.

While it is clear that the extension of insurance by industry must come slowly, that an immediate start should be made in this extension seems equally unquestionable. Although the development is fraught with obvious difficulties and objections, it is not apparent that any of these are insuperable. It *is* apparent that State-operated unemployment insurance has reached a dead center where only inertia serves to carry it on. Insurance by industry on a wide scale is not only in all probability entirely feasible. It is a development as full of promise as the record of State-operated unemployment insurance is full of disillusionment.

The new policy must be evolved cautiously. It cannot be hastily thrown into action as long as unemployment remains far above normal. There is, however, no valid reason why a number of industries of low unemployment should not be encouraged to set up their Special Schemes forthwith.  To maintain the legislative ban on their doing so until the present deficiency in the National Unemployment Fund has been cleared up is absurd.  And the immediate steps in forwarding insurance by industry which can be taken now should be steadily improved upon as prosperity returns.

The lessons of unemployment are learned during periods of bad trade.  The time to apply those lessons successfully is in periods of good trade.  If the machinery of unemployment relief is not thoroughly revised and improved when employment is good, nothing will be gained by criticizing its ineffectiveness when trade is bad.

# APPENDIXES

# APPENDIX I

## THE SCOPE OF COMPULSORY UNEMPLOY-
## MENT INSURANCE AS ESTABLISHED BY
## THE ACT OF 1920

SUBJECT to the exceptions specified in Part II below, all persons of the age of sixteen and upwards who are engaged in any of the employments covered by Part I below are insured against unemployment in the manner provided by this Act.

### PART I. EMPLOYMENTS WITHIN THE MEANING OF THE ACT

(a) Employment in the United Kingdom under any contract of service or apprenticeship, written or oral, whether expressed or implied, and whether the employed person is paid by the employer or some other person, and whether under one or more employers, and whether paid by time or by the piece, or partly by time and partly by the piece, or otherwise, or, except in the case of a contract of apprenticeship, without any money payment.

, (b) Employment under such a contract as aforesaid as master or a member of the crew of any ship registered in the United Kingdom or of any other British ship or vessel of which the owner, or, if there is more than one owner, the managing owner or manager, resides or has his principal place of business in the United Kingdom.

(c) Employment under any local or other public authority, other than any such employment as may be excluded by a special order.

### PART II. EXCEPTED EMPLOYMENTS

(a) Employment in agriculture, including horticulture and forestry.

(b) Employment in domestic service, except where the employed person is employed in any trade or business carried on for the purposes of gain.

(c) Employment in the naval, military, or air service of the Crown, including service in officers' training corps, except as otherwise provided in this Act.

(d) Employment —
  (i) under any local or other public authority; or
  (ii) in a police force; or
  (iii) in the service of any railway company, or a joint committee of two or more such companies; or
  (iv) in the service of any public utility company, that is to say, any company carrying on any undertaking for the supply of gas, water, hydraulic power or electricity, any dock or canal undertaking, or any tramway undertaking, including a light railway constructed wholly or mainly on a public road; or
  (v) in which the persons employed are entitled to rights in a superannuation fund established by or in pursuance of an Act of Parliament for the benefit of persons in that employment,

where the Minister certifies that the employed person is not subject to dismissal except for misconduct or for neglect in the performance of or unfitness to perform his duties, and that the terms and conditions on which the employed person is engaged make it unnecessary that he should be insured under this Act.

(e) Employment as a teacher of any person who is in recognized service within the meaning of the School Teachers (Superannuation) Act, 1918, or in a capacity which, if that person were under the age of sixty-five years, would be such recognized service, or employment as a teacher to whom the scheme under the Education (Scotland) (Superannuation) Act, 1919, or the National School Teachers (Ireland) Act, 1879, applies, or, in the event of any similar enactment being hereafter passed as respects teachers or any class of teachers, as a teacher to whom such enactment applies.

(f) Employment as a teacher in a State-aided school in Scotland at any time after the person employed has undergone an examination in order to qualify for the position of a certificated teacher and before the announcement of the result of the examination, and employment as a junior student in such a school, and employment in a public elementary school in England as a pupil or student teacher or in a national school in Ireland as a monitor.

(g) Employment as an agent paid by commission or fees or a share in the profits, or partly in one and partly in another such ways, where the person so employed is mainly dependent for his livelihood on his earnings from some other occupation, or where he is ordinarily employed as such agent by more than one employer, and his employment under no one of such employers is that on which he is mainly dependent for his livelihood.

(h) Employment otherwise than by way of manual labor and at a rate of remuneration exceeding in value two hundred and fifty pounds a year, or in cases where such employment involves part-time service only, at a rate of remuneration which, in the opinion of the Minister, is equivalent to a rate of remuneration exceeding two hundred and fifty pounds a year for whole-time service.

(i) Employment of a casual nature otherwise than for the purposes of the employer's trade or business, and otherwise than for the purposes of any game or recreation where the persons employed are engaged or paid through a club, and in such cases the club shall be deemed to be the employer.

(j) Employment of any class which may be specified in a special order made by the Minister, or in a special order made under the National Insurance Health Acts, 1911 to 1920, and declared by the Minister to apply for the purposes of this Act, as being of such a nature that it is ordinarily adopted as subsidiary employment only and not as the principal means of livelihood.

(k) Employment as a member of the crew of a fishing vessel where the employed person is wholly remunerated by a share in the profits or the gross earnings of the working of the vessel.

(l) Employment in the service of the husband or wife of the employed person.

(m) Employment in respect of which no wages or other money payment is made, where the person employed is the child of, or is maintained by, the employer.

Since the passage of the Act of 1920 it has been found advisable to except a very few uncommon employments, insurable under the major Act. The most important of these is the occupation of "female nurses for the sick," excepted by Section 10 of the Act of April, 1922.

# APPENDIX II

## SECTIONS (18 TO 21, INCLUSIVE) OF THE ACT OF 1920 PROVIDING THE POWER TO INITIATE UNEMPLOYMENT INSURANCE BY INDUSTRY

18. — (1) If it appears to the Minister that insurance against unemployment in any industry can be more satisfactorily provided for by a scheme under this Section than by the general provisions of this Act, the Minister may, subject to the provisions of this Section, approve or make such a scheme, and any such scheme is in this Act referred to as "a special scheme."

(2) The Minister may by special order approve for the purposes of this Section, and whether with or without amendment, any scheme which is made in respect of any industry by a joint industrial council or an association of employers and employees and which provides for the insurance against unemployment of all the employed persons in the industry, or all those persons other than any specified classes thereof, and the benefits under which are in the opinion of the Minister not less favorable on the whole than the benefits provided by this Act.

(3) Provision may be made by a special scheme for insuring persons to whom the scheme applies against partial unemployment as well as against unemployment.

(4) Where no special scheme has been made with respect to an industry by a joint industrial council or association of employers and employees and approved by the Minister, the Minister after consultation with the joint industrial council or with persons representing the employers and employees who would be affected by the scheme may himself by special order make a special scheme with respect to that industry.

(5) A special scheme shall not apply to any persons other than persons who are employed persons within the meaning of this Act.

(6) Where a special scheme is in force, the employed persons to whom the scheme applies shall not, subject to the provisions of this Act, be liable to become or to continue to be insured under the general provisions of this Act, or be entitled to unemployment benefit.

(7) Where a special scheme is in force, there shall, subject to compliance with the prescribed conditions, be paid to the body charged with the administration of the scheme in every year out of moneys provided by Parliament such sum as the Minister, in view of the estimated income and expenditure under the scheme, may by regulations made by him with the consent of the Treasury determine but not exceeding in any event three-tenths of the amount, calculated in the prescribed manner, which would, if the scheme had not been in force, have been paid by way of contributions under the general provisions of this Act out of moneys provided by Parliament in respect of the employed persons to whom the scheme applies.

(8) A special scheme may apply for the purposes of the scheme, with or without modification, any of the provisions of this Act, and may contain such other provisions, including provisions for the constitution of a body to be charged with the administration of the scheme and with respect to the supervision of the administration of the scheme and accounts, and, subject to the consent of the Treasury, with respect to the investment of funds and audit, as the Minister considers to be necessary for the purpose of giving effect to the scheme and to the provisions of this Section:

The general provisions of this Act shall not, except in so far as they are applied by a special scheme, apply to, or have effect in relation to or for the purposes of, any special scheme or the persons insured thereunder.

(9) A special scheme shall, when approved or made by the Minister, have effect as if enacted in this Act and shall continue in force until determined in accordance with the provisions thereof, and the Minister may at any time, in the case of a special scheme made by a joint industrial council or an association of employers and employees on the application of the council or association, and in the case of a scheme made by himself after consultation with persons representing employers and employees affected by the scheme, by special order vary or amend the provisions of a scheme made under this Section.

(10) Where a special scheme for any industry comes into force on or before the fourth day of July, nineteen hundred and twenty-one, there shall be paid out of the unemployment fund to the body charged with the administration of the scheme such sum as may be determined to be approximately equivalent to the amount of the contributions paid by employers and employed persons during the period between the commencement of this Act and the date on which the scheme comes into force in respect of employed persons while employed in the industry, together with such sum

as may be determined to be approximately equivalent to the amount to which, having regard to the number of the contributions aforesaid, the body charged with the administration of the scheme would if the scheme had been in force during the period aforesaid have been entitled under subsection (7) of this Section, after deducting such sum as may be determined to be approximately equivalent to the amount paid or payable out of the unemployment fund to employed persons in the industry at any time before they cease to be entitled to benefit under the general provisions of this Act, together with such sum as may be determined to be approximately equivalent to the rateable part of the costs of administering the general provisions of this Act.

In this subsection the expression "determined" means determined in accordance with regulations made under this Act by the Minister with the approval of the Treasury.

(11) A special scheme may be made with respect to two or more industries, and in relation to a scheme so made or proposed to be so made this section shall have effect as if for the references therein to a joint industrial council or an association of employers and employees there were substituted references to joint industrial councils or associations of employers and employees acting in respect of the two or more industries.

(12) For the purposes of this section —

The expression "industry" means any class or classes of establishments or undertakings, or any class or classes of establishments or undertakings in any area, which the Minister may determine to be an industry for that purpose; and

The expression "association of employers and employees" means an association so constituted that the members of the association who are employers consist of persons employing a substantial majority of the employees in the industry and the members who are employees consist of persons representing a substantial majority of the employees in the industry; and

A person shall be deemed, notwithstanding that he is employed on any day, to be partially unemployed if on that day the employment available for him is not such as to enable him to earn the full rate of wages, and the expression "partial unemployment" shall be construed accordingly.

### Transition to Special Schemes

19. — The Minister may, with the approval of the Treasury, make regulations for determining and regulating the position of

persons who at any time pass from the general provisions of this
Act to the provisions of a special scheme, or from the provisions
of a special scheme to the general provisions of this Act, or from
one special scheme to another special scheme, and in particular
for providing that a person shall be entitled, for such period and
subject to such terms and conditions as may be specified by or
in pursuance of the regulations, to receive unemployment benefit
under this Act, or benefits under a special scheme after he has
ceased to be subject to the general provisions of this Act or to
the scheme, as the case may be.

## SUPPLEMENTARY SCHEMES

20. — (1) A joint industrial council or an association of employers and employees may submit to the Minister a scheme for
insuring insured contributors in any industry against unemployment during periods of unemployment in respect of which they
may not be entitled to unemployment benefit or against partial
unemployment, or for paying to any such insured contributors
while they are in receipt of unemployment benefit an additional
sum by way of benefit in respect of unemployment.

(2) The Minister may by special order approve, whether with
or without amendment, any scheme so submitted (in this Act
referred to as a "supplementary scheme") if he is satisfied that
it is expedient that the scheme should come into operation.

(3) A supplementary scheme may apply, for the purposes of
the scheme, with or without modifications, any of the provisions
of this Act, and may contain such other provisions (including
provisions for the constitution of a body to be charged with the
administration of the scheme and with respect to the supervision
of the administration of the scheme and accounts) as the Minister
considers to be necessary for the purpose of giving effect to the
scheme:

Provided that —

  (a) no part of the funds required for providing benefits
      under a supplementary scheme or otherwise in con-
      nection therewith shall be derived from moneys pro-
      vided by Parliament; and

  (b) the general provisions of this Act shall not, except in
      so far as they are applied by a supplementary scheme,
      apply to or have effect in relation to or for the pur-
      poses of the scheme.

(4) A supplementary scheme, when approved by the Minister,
shall have effect as if enacted in this Act and shall continue in
force until determined in accordance with the provisions thereof,

and the Minister may at any time if so requested by the joint industrial council or association of employers and employees concerned by special order vary or amend the provisions of the scheme.

(5) In this section the expressions "industry" and "association of employers and employees" and "partial unemployment" have respectively the same meanings as in the provisions of this Act relating to special schemes.

## POWER TO REQUIRE STATISTICS

21. — The Minister may make regulations requiring the body charged with the administration of a special scheme, or of a supplementary scheme, to furnish at prescribed intervals returns with respect to the state of employment in the industry to which the scheme relates, and with respect to such other matters in connection with the scheme as may be prescribed.

# APPENDIX III

## SAMPLE DECISION BY THE UMPIRE

(Case No. 4205; Decision rendered under the statutory condition that a recipient of unemployment benefit be "capable of and available for work, but unable to obtain suitable employment," as provided in Section 7 (I) (iii) of the Act of 1920.)

THE applicant, whose usual occupation was that of an engineer, reported at the Swindon Employment Exchange on 4th December, 1922, and asked that his claim for benefit should be transferred to that office from the Birmingham Exchange. He had left Birmingham on 19th November, 1922.

He stated that he was travelling about the country with his wife, who was a member of a theatrical touring company, which was performing in Swindon during that week, and he would be proceeding to Bath with the company in the following week. He submitted that he was improving his prospects of securing work by travelling about, and, in the event of his being able to secure work anywhere, he would accept it.

*Recommended* by the Court of Referees that the claim for benefit should be allowed.

The Insurance Officer declined to accept the recommendation. He did not think the applicant satisfied the conditions of Section 7 (I) (iii), while touring the country. The fact that the applicant remained only one week in any particular town made it almost impossible for the Employment Exchanges to keep in touch with him for the purpose of offering work.

*Decision.* — "On the facts before me my decision is that the claim for benefit should be disallowed.

"The applicant, who is an engineer by trade, cannot, in my opinion, be held to be available for work while he is travelling about the country with a touring theatrical company."

# APPENDIX IV

## SPECIMEN SHEET OF NATIONAL CLEARING HOUSE GAZETTE

# Vacancies for Women.

401    402    403

## 076. FRENCH POLISHER.

0762. 522—FARNWORTH. 39, FRENCH POLISHER. For furniture. Able to mix own polish colour perm. S.R 1s 6d. p.h. 47 h.p.w Fare pd. reas. dist. R. Shepherd. Exp. poss. Temp., T.U pref.

*There is a general demand throughout the United Kingdom for Domestic Servants of all types, e.g., Cooks, Cook-generals, Parlourmaids, Housemaids. If an applicant wishes to obtain a post as a Domestic Servant in any particular part of the United Kingdom, she should apply at the counter when particulars of her qualifications, etc., will be submitted for any vacancies that may be available.*

150. RESIDENT SERVANTS IN HOTELS, BOARDING HOUSES, EATING HOUSES, etc.

151. RESIDENT DOMESTIC SERVANTS IN PRIVATE HOUSES, COLLEGES, INSTITUTIONS, etc.—contd.

151. RESIDENT DOMESTIC SERVANTS IN PRIVATE HOUSES, COLLEGES, INSTITUTIONS, etc.—contd.

**....82-LETCHWORTH. 24.**
1 RESTAURANT COOK. Thoro. exp. in plain cookg. Age 30-35 pref. Perm. £40 p.a. Resi. Hrs. 74. To cook abt. 80 luncheons p.d. Share bedroom with housemaid. Fare pd. 12 or 13 staff. F. Nott.

**15616. 288-WEYMOUTH. 355/1.**
1 COOK Commercial hotel. Exp. Age 30-40. Perm. £1 p.w. Adv. & deduct; refund after 3 mos. Kitchenmaid kept. Share bedroom. Crown hotel.

**15616. 880-PEMBROKE DOCK. 22/1.**
1 HOTEL COOK. Exp. Perm. £1 p.w. Fare pd. Share bedroom. Unif. not necess. Edinburgh Hotel.

**15612. 168-ST. ALBANS. 25.**
1 GENERAL (Housewrk.) Some exp. Perm. £30. Sep. room. Fare arrgd. Not too old. No unif. req. Ref. No applics. over 60 miles dist. Verulam Arms.

**15618. 605-OLDHAM. 2/2.**
1 HOTEL GENERAL. Exp. To assist in bar. Perm. 15s. p.w. Share bedroom. Fare pd. reas. dist. 2 in fam. Old Sergeant.

**15624. 288-WEYMOUTH. 195/8.**
1 HOUSEMAID-WAITRESS. Private hotel. Exp. Perm. 12s. 6d. p.w. Adv. & deduct; refund after 3 mos. Share bedroom. Unif. necess. (no caps). 7 maids and 1 boy. Crescent Hotel.

**15624. 288-WEYMOUTH. 428/1.**
1 HOUSEMAID-WAITRESS. For boarding-house. Exp. Perm. 12s. 6d. p.w. Adv. & deduct; refund after 3 mos. Share bedroom. 2 maids. Av. no. people, 30. Usual unif. "La Touraine".

**15625. 222-KING'S LYNN. 78.**
1 KITCHENMAID. Hotel. Healthy looking. Season. 15s. p.w. Refs. with "H" form. Share bedroom. Fare pd. Glebe Hotel, Hunstanton.

**15628. 282-WEYMOUTH. 203/8.**
1 LINEN-MAID. High-class hotel. Exp. Age, 25-30. Refs. Perm. 16s. to 17s. p.w. Fare pd. Share bedroom. Royal Hotel.

**15630. 222-KING'S LYNN. 79.**
1 PANTRY MAID. Hotel exp. Healthy looking. Season. 12s.-15s. p.w. accord. to exp. Refs, if poss, with "H" form. Adv. & deduct. Share bedroom. Glebe Hotel, Hunstanton.

**15632. 288-WEYMOUTH. 64/2.**
1 STILLROOM-MAID. Exp. Age, 20-25. Perm. 12s. 6d. to 15s. p.w. able. Fare pd. Share bedroom. Usual unif. Large staff. Trocadero Restaurant.

**15116. 289-WINCHESTER. 13/2.**
1 COOK (good plain). Girls' High School Boarding House. Able to cook for 30-40. Perm. £45-£50 p.a. Fare pd. Share room. Miss Guyer, North Hill House.

**15116. 289-WINCHESTER. 73.**
1 COOK (plain). Girls' High School Boarding House. Not too young. Used to numbers (30-40). Perm. £40-£45 p.a. Own room. Fare pd. for interview and on taking up employment. Miss Weston.

**15116. 297-TAUNTON. 65.**
1 COOK. Exp. Perm. £40 p.a. House parlourmaid and ketchenmaid kept. Fare arrgd. Taunton Stn. Mrs. Greenslade, Trull.

**15116. 856-BIRKENHEAD. 259.**
1 COOK. Exp. Age 28-35. Perm. £50. Gd. outs. Refs. Unif. 2 maids. Share bedroom. 5 in fam. Fare pd.

**15118. 160-ST. ALBANS. 36.**
1 COOK-GENERAL. Exp. Refs. Perm. £40. Probably share bedroom. Fares arrgd. £45.

**15118. 192-LETCHWORTH. 66.**
1 COOK-GENERAL OR HOUSEKEEPER. Plain cookg. Thor. capable and able to undertake all household duties. Perm. £1 p.w. without help (resident); and £? p.a. if help is given. Own bedroom. Unif. not necess. Fare pd. reas. dist. 6 in fam. (no chldrn.). Widow be considered. Mrs. Booth, Baldock.

**15118. 192-LETCHWORTH. 61.**
1 COOK-GENERAL. Exp. plain cooking. Perm. £40 p.a. Lib. outs. Sep. bedroom. Apps. within 70 miles radius only considered. Unif. essen. Fare pd. 4 in fam. See Order 15132=192=74. Mother and daughter or two friends would suit.

**15118. 536-CHESTER. 24.**
1 COOK-GENERAL. Exp. Perm. £40 p.a. Sep. bedroom. Gd. outs. Fare pd. reas. dist. 2 maids.

**15118. 536-CHESTER. 115.**
1 COOK-GENERAL. Exp. Willing to do washg. Perm. £40. Gd. outs. Sep. bedroom. Employer would pay fare reas. dist. 4 chldrn.

**15118. 578-LEVENSHULME. 1331.**
1 COOK-GENERAL. Exp. Perm. £50 p.a. 7 in fam. incld. 4 chldrn. Nurse and 3 maids kept. Share bedroom. Do own washg. Gd. outs. Fare arrgd. "H" forms to Withington B.O. Jewish fam. Mrs. Shobet, Didsbury

**15118. 658-STOCKPORT. 84.**
1 COOK-GENERAL. Exp. Perm. £45 p.a. Unif. prov. Housemaid. Daily help and boy kept. Fare arrgd. Sep. bedroom. The Matron,

**15126. 578-LEVENSHULME. 68.**
1 HOUSE-PARLOURMAID. Exp. at table. Perm. £36-£40. 4 in fam. Cook-gen. and house-maid. Share bedroom. Gd. outs. Fare pd. reas. dist. "H" forms to Withington B.O. Young, Withington

**15126. 579-MACCLESFIELD. 68.**
1 HOUSE-PARLOURMAID. Exp. No rough wrk. No wash. Perm. £45 p.a. Sep. bedroom. Unif. req. Fare pd. Lib. outs. Scotch pref. Mrs.

**15128. 4-GT. MARLBOROUGH ST. 5887.**
1 KITCHENMAID. Fever hospital. Able do plain cookg. Perm. £48 ins. + £18 W.B. 48 h.p.w. Board, lodg. and unif prov. Adv. & deduct. Refunded after 3 mos.' satis. service. Copy of undertaking to repay must be forwarded to E.E. same day as applicant travels. "H" forms, copies of 2 refs. and med. cert. with written applic. to E.E. M.A.B.

**15128. 10-DARTFORD. 31.**
1 KITCHENMAID. Single or widow. Age 18-35. Perm. 30s. p.w., rising to 34s. Gd. p.w. + pres. bonus 15s. 6d. p.w. 96 h.p. fortnight. Uniform free after 3 mos. Lodg. and meals charged for. Pensionable. No fares. "H" forms to E.E. L.C. Mental Hospital, Bexley.

**15128. 578-LEVENSHULME. 251.**
1 KITCHENMAID. Hostel for women students. Knowl. of plain cookg. Perm. £30 (to begin). 13 maids. Unif. reqd. Share bedroom. Lib. outs. Bd. wages in hols. Fare pd. reas. dist. "H" forms to Withington B.O. The Warden, Ashburne Hall, Fallowfield.

**15128. 580-MANCHESTER. 896.**
1 SENIOR KITCHENMAID. Exp. in institution wrk. Perm. £50. Share bedroom. No fares. Ancoats Hospital

**15132. 175-ALDERSHOT. 558.**
1 NURSE. Exp. Entire charge of baby. 2 yrs. Perm. 16s. p.w. Share bedroom with baby. Fare pd. for int. if reqd. Indoor unif. reqd. Refs. with "H" form. Mrs. Cohen, Princess Hotel.

**15132. 192-LETCHWORTH. 74.**
1 CHILDREN'S NURSE. Exp. Thor. used to children. Perm. £30-£35 p.a. Lib. outs. Share night nursery with children. Apps. within 70 miles radius considered. Fare pd. 4 in fam. including 3 children. Unif. req. See Order No. 15118-192-61. Mother and daughter or two friends would suit

**15136. 281-COWES, I.O.W. 75.**
1 PARLOURMAID. Able to valet well. Single-handed. Exp. Perm. £30-£36 p.a. Sep. bedroom. Fare pd. 5 maids kept.

**15142. 28-SUTTON. 123.**
1 MESSROOM ASSISTANT. Single or widow.

# APPENDIX V

## "PRODUCTIVE" RELIEF WORK IN POST-WAR GERMANY [1]

THE substitution of employment on public works for the payment of doles was early recognized by the Republican Ministry of Labor as advisable from every viewpoint. From the beginning of the new regime State doles for the unemployed have been regarded as a makeshift. The problem for the Ministry of Labor was to find a constructive substitute for the system of unemployment doles, and an initial effort at solution was made by an Act passed at the beginning of 1920 giving this Ministry authority to subsidize *produktive Erwerbslosenfürsorge* from the public Treasury in order to relieve unemployment.

At first narrowly limited in its scope, the law was shortly expanded to cover any project manifestly in the public interest. Statistics indicate the extent of the experiment. During the first six months of operation (May 1 to November 1, 1920) 2400 contracts, with a total expense of 375,000,000 marks,[2] were let by the Federal Government, States, and municipalities. By October 1, 1921, over 9000 contracts had been let. During the first five months of 1921 an average of 230,000 formerly unemployed were continuously engaged in productive work under this legislation. In other words, as the total number of completely workless in Germany receiving doles during this period averaged a little over 420,000, the program of productive unemployment relief was then cutting down subsidized unemployment by thirty-five per cent.[3]

In nature and in extent the German public works undertakings cover a wide variety. Contract No. 8976, granted to the hamlet of Eibenberg on June 27th, 1921, was for repairs to the village street, occupied four otherwise unemployed workers for nineteen days, and cost a total of 8039 marks (then about thirty pounds).

[1] The description is of the program as it was operating during 1921. A similar system was introduced in Austria in October, 1922, and is said by the Austrian Minister of Social Welfare to have proved that productive unemployment relief is an efficient method of combating unemployment.

[2] During the period under survey the mark remained fairly stable at a rate averaging about two hundred to the pound, or forty-five to the dollar.

[3] The number of those engaged in "productive relief work" is from an announcement of the Federal Minister of Labor, quoted by Weck in *Die Erwerbslosenfürsorge*, p. 67. The other figures are taken from the bi-monthly official *Reichs-Arbeitsblatt*.

Contract No. 9031, granted the city of Leipzig on June 22nd, 1921, was to carry out a flood-regulation project near the city. It gave work to 200 otherwise unemployed for 225 days each, at a total estimated cost of 9,000,000 marks. The greatest single productive unemployment relief undertaking in Germany to date is the highway system being constructed over the Jura mountains. This immense project, designed to bring Bavaria and North Germany into closer contact, is giving work to three thousand unemployed, and was two-thirds completed at the end of August, 1921. Another big undertaking, which any visitor to Berlin will literally stumble upon before he has been in the city a day, is the Friedrichstrasse underground railway, started before the war, abandoned for five years, and now resumed as a *produktive* contract. A public hospital is being constructed in Berlin in the same manner. In fact, from irrigation, canal building and electrification projects to street paving and the repair and construction of workers' dwellings, there is hardly a type of undertaking of public benefit which has not been already included in the public works program.

While the municipalities are carrying out many of these public works projects under the management of public officials, private contractors have been selected to handle the work in almost all of the larger undertakings. That this policy, when adequately safeguarded by the State, is the more economical and the more efficient under present conditions is frankly admitted by Socialists in charge of the productive work program. In launching a project the procedure adheres to the following general lines. The municipality, which is customarily the applicant for the subsidy, submits full particulars of the work to be undertaken, together with estimates of cost. Approval or disapproval rests with the Ministry of Labor, which, in all cases involving large expenditure, institutes careful inquiries to see whether the construction desired is of economic and public value, whether the estimates submitted are reasonable, and whether the unemployment situation in the locality in question is sufficiently serious to warrant the enterprise as a relief undertaking. If the Federal Government is satisfied, it grants the municipality a subsidy equal to three-sixths of the cost of the undertaking, two-sixths having to be provided by the State concerned and one-sixth by the municipality itself. Once assurance of the subsidy is secured, the local town council or other public body is free either to go ahead with the work itself, or to accept the most favorable bid of the competing private contractors.

A most interesting feature of the *produktive Erwerbslosenfürsorge* is the plan which has been evolved to ensure that these activities shall give work to *bona fide* unemployed. The contractor, in the interest of efficiency, is allowed to gather a certain percentage of the necessary labor himself. These *Stammarbeiter*, or key men, generally workers who have been associated with the firm in other projects and of proved ability and responsibility, are placed by the contractor in the positions where men of known experience are necessary. The number of *Stammarbeiter* allowed varies slightly, but generally in Prussia it is 20 per cent of the total employed. For the Friedrichstrasse subway, a piece of construction demanding a large proportion of unskilled or semi-skilled workers, it is only 16 per cent. Whenever the contractor can show that it is vital to the work to have a larger number of known workers, that larger percentage will be allowed.

So far the procedure in starting construction is much the same as that customarily followed by the private contractor who starts a building job with a nucleus of proved men, and then hires and "fires" masses of casual labor as he proceeds with the undertaking. At the point where the casual-labor problem first makes itself felt in ordinary private operations comes the safeguard in this German experiment. The four-fifths or five-sixths of the employees who in ordinary operations would be engaged by the private contractor at the gate, or by advertising, or perhaps through an Employment Exchange, must in the German relief works program be taken on through the public Employment Exchanges. That labor should be secured in this way is as much a part of the contract as the price which is to be paid for the job. And should it seem necessary to discharge a man taken on in this manner, a "right" of the employer which the Works Councils are empowered to overrule if it is being exercised unjustly, not only must the employer give reasons for the discharge to the Employment Exchanges, but he must also hire any man taken on in place of the discharged employee through the same agency.

At least since the historic French failure of 1848, it has been argued that labor employed on public works for relief purposes is inefficient, and carefully the conclusion has been built up that such projects are a form of interference with private enterprise which should be allowed only a spasmodic development in cases of the most urgent need. An outstanding characteristic of the German unemployment policy is that there is nothing spasmodic in any of its experiments, and aside from the obvious benefits of keeping unemployment at a minimum, stimulating business, and accomplishing useful work, it is apparent that the public works program is developing successfully as a part of permanent policy. The combination of Capitalist and Socialist philosophy involved appears to be a happy one. The contractor is an experienced business man who must bid low to get the contract, and who must manage efficiently to keep it. The labor which is provided through the exchanges is not an unknown, casual quantity, as is inevitably the case with gate and foreman hiring, but is in each instance a registered man with every incentive for keeping his industrial record as good as possible. If he is familiar with the work to which he is sent, he gets the standard trade-union wages; if it is new work for him, he is at least assured of a living, while every opportunity is given him to learn. He cannot be "fired" without the employer showing good reason why. Both as an individual and as a member of his union, he knows that the better his job is done the more work of like nature will be available later. The worker is protected in his employment and guarded from the terrible demoralization of continued unemployment; the employer is furnished with business, and hampered only in so far as he is forced to treat his employees as human beings with a position in the State as worthy of protection as is his own; the State, and through it the general public, benefits by the cheap and efficient provision of works which are of proved necessity and real public benefit.

# APPENDIX VI

## EMERGENCY EMPLOYMENT MEASURES IN GREAT BRITAIN

THE following account summarizes the emergency measures supplemental to the main program undertaken by the British Government in the years 1921–23 to provide alternative employment, to encourage the development and restoration of foreign trade, and to stimulate enterprises likely to give employment to workpeople in Great Britain. Most of these measures owe their origin to conferences of the Unemployment Committee of the Cabinet which was instituted early in the depression, during the Lloyd George Premiership, to keep close watch on the critical situation aroused by wholesale unemployment.

### TRADE STIMULATION SCHEMES

By the Trade Facilities Act of 1921 the Treasury was empowered to guarantee, up to a total of £25,000,000, payment of the interest and principal of loans raised by any public authority or other body of persons in order to carry out undertakings calculated to promote employment in Great Britain and Ireland. In the following year the Trade Facilities and Loans Guarantee Act sanctioned increase of the aggregate capital amount of loans which might be guaranteed to £50,000,000. This in turn was raised to £65,000,000 in May, 1924. Guarantees actually given or sanctioned up to September 13, 1923, amounted to a total of £29,469,645.

The Export Credits Scheme, initiated in 1921, allows the Government to grant credits and undertake insurance for the purpose of re-establishing British overseas trade. The guarantee may be as great as 100 per cent of the cost, with recourse against the exporter for 57½ per cent only. Credits may be sanctioned up to £26,000,000, and a large proportion of that amount has at one time or another been involved. The credits are in constant circulation, the completion of one scheme releasing the credit involved and making it free for the guarantee of another. On September 10, 1923, the amount of credit actually in use was £11,249,394, leaving an available balance on that date of £14,750,606.

### RELIEF WORKS

The Ministry of Transport makes grants to Local Authorities up to fifty per cent of the total cost involved in respect of approved highway construction and improvement undertakings. A usual condition of these grants is that the work shall be done in winter-time, in order to absorb as much as possible of the seasonal unemployment of that period. During the three winters from the Autumn of 1920 to the Spring of 1923 contributions were offered through the Road Fund to schemes having a total cost of approximately £27,000,000. It was estimated that schemes in progress during the financial year 1923–24 would entail a total expenditure of £7,500,000, representing approximately a full year's work for 27,000 men. The Ministry of Transport also undertook to provide half the cost of two light railways, costing £325,000, which were started during the winter of 1921–22.

, Various emergency works of wide variety, though somewhat more narrow in scope than those embodied in the German program, were undertaken by the National and Local Governments from the Autumn of 1920 onwards. At various times at least 300,000 unemployed have been found work in these projects, about 130,000 being directly employed on them in September, 1923. The great majority of those found employment on relief works of one form or another are taken on through the agency of the Employment Exchanges.

### Agriculture and Forestry Schemes

The Ministry of Agriculture and Fisheries assisted Drainage Authorities throughout the depression with land drainage schemes primarily intended to provide productive work for the unemployed in agriculture. In these cases the whole of the approved cost was advanced, and a proportion refunded by the authorities on the completion of the scheme. Undertakings to supply or improve the supply of water to farms were also assisted, but here grants were made to cover only a part of the cost. Up to the Spring of 1923 schemes costing nearly £800,000 were approved under this heading, of which about one-quarter was recoverable.

The Forestry Commission assisted works of afforestation during the winters 1921–22 and 1922–23 in free grants, amounting to about sixty per cent of the labor costs, to the extent of about £200,000. The normal program of planting and preparation was increased by the Forestry Commissioners as a minor part of the Government emergency relief program.

### Acceleration of Government Contracts

Various Government Departments, particularly the Post Office, the War Office and the Admiralty, accelerated their contract work during the winter months of the depression period with a view to providing employment. Effort was also made to concentrate expenditure in areas where unemployment was particularly severe. For example, during the winter of 1923–24 the Post Office Department entered upon a program of laying additional trunk telephone cables with an estimated cost of £500,000.

## UNEMPLOYMENT GRANTS COMMITTEE

The work of this special emergency committee during the depression has been the most skillfully planned of the whole emergency program. As its work developed the Unemployment Grants Committee devoted particular attention to furthering employment for skilled workmen in their normal occupations, thereby doing something to meet the objection that ordinary relief works are useless, except as task work, for most skilled workers out of employment. But the problem of furthering work for unemployed women by these schemes proved difficult of solution.

Up to the winter of 1923–24 the Committee sanctioned expenditures by Local Authorities amounting to approximately £30,000,000 on the basis that the State would repay a part of the wages bill of works normally defrayed out of revenue, or part of the interest on loans raised for revenue producing schemes. Certain other assistance also was available.[1]

For the winter of 1923–24 the Government increased the scope of these grants by extending financial assistance to private enterprise willing to commence revenue-producing works similar to those undertaken by Local Authorities which would otherwise have been postponed. Assistance was limited to a maximum of 50 per cent of interest at an approved rate on the expenditure, the grant being made for a period of years dependent on the extent to which the work was accelerated and the date at which the completed work would become remunerative. Only works of a public utility character, — gas, water, electricity, tramways, docks, harbors and canals — were assisted. Among other provisos[2] the terms of contracts for assisted undertakings had to be approved by the Committee, and all materials employed must be of British manufacture.

It has been officially estimated that the total program of emergency relief outlined in this appendix provided direct employment for about 200,000 who would otherwise have been workless during the winter of 1923–24.

[1] Full particulars of grants made by the Unemployment Grants Committee can be obtained from the Secretary, 23 Buckingham Gate, London, S.W. 1.
[2] See the *Labor Gazette*, October, 1923, p. 360, for full list of terms.

# SOURCES

# SOURCES

THE following list of books, pamphlets, journals, articles, legislation, and reports does not purport to be a bibliography of British Unemployment Relief. Indeed, a few of the writings mentioned have an apparently remote connection with the subject. The effort has been made, however, to note down hereunder all printed sources which have been of fairly direct value in the making of this study. But a large part of the material has been gathered by the author piecemeal, from personal investigation of the British system of unemployment relief.

Place of publication is London, unless otherwise stated. Dates given are those of editions used.

## SECTION I. UNOFFICIAL PUBLICATIONS

### A — BOOKS

BARKER, ERNEST. *Political Thought in England*, 1916.

BEER, M. *A History of British Socialism*, 1920.

BEVERIDGE, W. H. *Unemployment*, 1917.

BURTON, T. E. *Financial Crises*, New York, 1902.

COHEN, J. L. *Insurance against Unemployment*, 1921.

COLE, G. D. H. *Guild Socialism Re-Stated*, 1920.

GREENWOOD, A. *Juvenile Labour Exchanges and After-Care*, 1911.

HAWTREY, R. G. *Good and Bad Trade*, 1913.

HOBSON, J. A. *The Evolution of Modern Capitalism*, 1919.
    *The Economics of Unemployment*, 1922.

HOBSON, S. G. *National Guilds and the State*, 1920.

HODGES, FRANK. *Nationalization of the Mines*, 1920.

HYNDMAN, H. M. *Commercial Crises of the Nineteenth Century*, 1892.

JACKSON, CYRIL. *Unemployment and Trade Unions*, 1910.

JONES, E. D. *Economic Crises*, New York, 1900.

KEELING, F. *The Labour Exchange in Relation to Boy and Girl Labour*, 1910.

KITSON, A. *Unemployment*, 1921.

KLEIN, PHILIP. *The Burden of Unemployment*, New York, 1923.

LAVINGTON, F. *The Trade Cycle*, 1922.

LAWRENCE, F. W. PETHICK. *Unemployment*, 1922.

LIPSON, E. *Increased Production*, 1922.

MACROSTY, W. H. *The Trust Movement in British Industry*, 1909.

MACGREGOR, D. H. *The Evolution of Industry*, 1911.

MESS, H. A. *Casual Labour at the Docks*, 1916.
MILL, J. S. *On Liberty*, 1912.
MITCHELL, WESLEY C. *Business Cycles*, Berkeley, 1913.
MONEY, L. CHIOZZA. *The Triumph of Nationalization*, 1920.
NATIONAL INDUSTRIAL ⎱ *Unemployment Insurance in Theory and*
CONFERENCE BOARD. ⎰ *Practise*, New York, 1922.
PENTY, A. J. *Guilds, Trade and Agriculture*, 1921.
PIGOU, A. C. *Unemployment*, 1913.
ROWNTREE, B. SEEBOHM. *The Way to Industrial Peace*, 1914.
TAWNEY, R. H. *The Acquisitive Society*, 1921.
VARIOUS AUTHORS. *The Third Winter of Unemployment*, 1922.
WEBB, SIDNEY. *Industrial Democracy*, 1913.
(Mr. and Mrs.) *The Prevention of Destitution*, 1916.
*The History of Trade Unionism*, 1920.
*A Constitution for the Socialist Commonwealth of
Great Britain*, 1920.
WECK, RUDOLF. *Die Erwerbslosenfürsorge*, Berlin, 1921.
WILLIAMS, R. *The Liverpool Docks Problem*, Liverpool, 1912.
*The First Year's Working of the Liverpool Docks
Scheme*, Liverpool, 1914.


B — ARTICLES, JOURNALS, AND PAMPHLETS

COLE, G. D. H. *Unemployment and Industrial Maintenance*, 1921.
HODGES, FRANK. *Workers' Control in the Coal-Mining Industry*,
1920.
LABOUR PARTY, THE. *The Prevention of Unemployment after the
War*, 1917.
*Unemployment, the Peace, and the Indemnity*,
1921.
*Unemployment, A Labour Policy*, 1921.
*Labour and the Unemployment Crisis*, 1921.
*Social Insurance and Trade Union Member-
ship*, 1923.
LABOUR RESEARCH DEPARTMENT. Monthly Circular (various
issues), 1921–22.
LANSBURY, GEORGE. "Poplar and the Labour Party," *Labour
Monthly*, June, 1922.
LESSER. HENRY. "Unemployment Insurance," *The Journal of
Industrial Administration*, 1922.
LLOYD, C. M. *The Present State of the Poor Law*, 1920.
MALLON, J. J. *Unemployment Insurance and Labour Exchanges
in England during and after the War*. Kölner
Vierteljahrshefte für Sozialwissenschaften, Col-
ogne, 1922.

MANCHESTER GUARDIAN COMMERCIAL. Special articles by:
Sir William Beveridge, February 1, 1923.
Lieutenant-Colonel D. C. McLagan, December 7, 1922.
A. V. Sugden, February 8, 1923.
G. F. Shove, February 8, 1923.
And other articles and reports in various issues of this journal
during 1921, 1922, and 1923.
MCKENNA, REGINALD. "The Problem of Unemployment," *Monthly
Review of the London Joint City and Mid-
land Bank*, January, 1922. (Also other
issues of this review.)
MORLEY, FELIX. "The Incidence of Unemployment by Age and
Sex," *The Economic Journal*, December, 1922.
"Unemployment Relief in Germany," *The Na-
tion and the Athenæum*, October 22, Novem-
ber 5 and 26, 1921.

NATIONAL TRANSPORT
WORKERS' FEDERATION. } Scheme drafted by Mr. Ernest Bevin
for maintenance of casual labour,
report of Eleventh Annual General
Council Meeting of the Federation,
Edinburgh, 1921.

VARIOUS AUTHORS. *Toynbee Hall Report on Unemployment in
East London*, 1922.

## SECTION II. OFFICIAL PUBLICATIONS

### GREAT BRITAIN

#### A — LEGISLATION

Unemployed Workmen Act, 1905.
Labour Exchanges Act, 1909.
National Insurance Act, 1911, Part II.
National Insurance (Part II Amendment) Act, 1914.
National Insurance (Part II) (Munition Workers) Act, 1916.
New Ministries and Secretaries Act, 1916.
National Insurance (Unemployment) Act, 1918.
National Insurance (Unemployment) Act, 1919.
Unemployment Insurance Act, 1920.
Unemployment Insurance (Temporary Provisions Amendment)
Act, 1920.
Unemployment (Relief Works) Act, 1920.
Unemployment Insurance Act, 1921.
Unemployment Insurance (No. 2) Act, 1921.

Unemployed Workers' Dependants (Temporary Provision) Act, 1921.
Trade Facilities Act.
Local Authorities (Financial Provisions) Act, 1921.
Poor Law Emergency-Provisions (Scotland) Act, 1921.
Unemployment Insurance Act, 1922.
Unemployment Insurance (No. 2) Act, 1922.
Unemployment Insurance Act, 1923.
Unemployment Insurance Acts of 1924.

### B — REPORTS, BLUE BOOKS, AND OTHER OFFICIAL PAPERS
#### (Arranged chronologically)

Report of the Royal Commission on the Poor Laws, Part II, 1909.
Minority Report of the Poor Law Commission (Parts I and II), 1909.
Report on Unemployment Insurance (Cd. 6965), 1913.
Report on Enquiry into Industrial Agreements (Cd. 6952), 1913.
Handbook for London Local Advisory Committees on Juvenile Employment, 1913.
Report of Committee on Trusts (Cd. 9236), 1919.
Report by a Court of Enquiry Concerning Wages and Conditions of Dock Labour, 1920.
Report of an Enquiry into the Conditions of Boy Labour on the Docks at Liverpool, 1920.
Report of the Committee of Enquiry into the Work of the Employment Exchanges (Cmd. 1054), 1920.
Minutes of Evidence before the Committee of Enquiry into the Work of the Employment Exchanges (Cmd. 1140), 1921.
Report by Viscount Chelmsford on Juvenile Employment, 1921.
Report of the Agricultural Wages Board Committee on Unemployment Insurance in Agriculture (Cmd. 1344), 1921.
Report by the Government Actuary on the Financial Provisions of the Unemployment Insurance (No. 2) Bill, 1921 (Cmd. 1336).
Rules of the Incorporated Insurance Industry Unemployment Insurance Board, 1921.
Report of the Oversea Settlement Committee for the Year Ended December 31, 1921 (Cmd. 1580), 1922.
Report by the Government Actuary on the Financial Provisions of the Unemployment Insurance Bill, 1922 (Cmd. 1620).
Report by the Inter-Departmental Committee on Health and Unemployment Insurance, 1922 (Cmd. 1644).
Report of Special Inquiry, under Direction of Minister of Health, into Expenditure of Poplar Board of Guardians, 1922.

Estimate for Civil Services for the Year Ending March 31, 1923, Class 7.

Third Interim Report of Inter-Departmental Committee on Health and Unemployment Insurance (Cmd. 1821), 1923.

Report on Administration of Section 18 of the Unemployment Insurance Act, 1920 (Cmd. 1613), 1923.

Memorandum on Financial Clauses of the Unemployment Insurance Act; 1923 (Cmd. 1824), 1923.

The Ministry of Labour *Gazette*, issues of January, 1920, to June, 1924 (inclusive).

Report on the Establishment and Progress of Joint Industrial Councils, 1917–22.

Report on National Unemployment Insurance to July, 1923.

## GERMANY

*Reichsverordnung über Erwerbslosenfürsorge* vom 26. Januar, 1920.

*Reichs-Gesetzblatt* (various dates of 1921 and 1922).

*Reichs-Arbeitsblatt* (bi-monthly issues from January, 1921 to December, 1922, inclusive).

*Arbeitsmarkt-Anzeiger* (various issues of 1921).

## UNITED STATES

*Business Cycles and Unemployment:* Report of a Committee of the President's Conference on Unemployment, 1923.

Wisconsin Bill on Reducing Unemployment, 1921.

*Monthly Labor Review*, Federal Bureau of Labor Statistics (various issues).

*The American Labor Legislation Review* (various issues). (Unofficial.)

The United States Employment Service; Institute for Government Research, Service Monograms of U. S. Government No. 28, 1923.

## LEAGUE OF NATIONS

(International Labor Office)

*British Legislation on Unemployment Insurance, Studies and Reports*, Series C, Geneva, 1920.

*Special Report on the Unemployment Inquiry*, Geneva, 1922.

*Remedies for Unemployment*, Geneva, 1922.

*Methods of Compiling Statistics of Unemployment*, Geneva, 1922.

*International Labor Review*, Geneva (various issues, 1922).

*Industrial and Labor Information*, Geneva (various issues, 1921–23).

# INDEX

Administrative expenses, 29, 96, 159.

Agriculture, unemployment insurance in, 35; unemployment relief in, 190.

Aliens, discrimination against in unemployment policy, 98.

Approved Societies, allowed to administer insurance benefit, 39 *et seq.*

Askwith, Lord, 7, 43.

Austria, productive unemployment relief in, 185.

Banking industry, special scheme, 46, 152.

Benefit, continuous, 60; highest rates under State-operated system, 53; inadequacy, 10, 20, 30, 37, 78, 146; rates proposed in April, 1924, 66.

Beveridge, Sir William H., 3, 8, 85, 90, 92, 138.

Branch Employment Offices, 99, 120.

Bureaucracy, defects of, 25, 77.

Chamberlain Circular, 1.

Claims and Record Office, 101, 120, 122.

Clynes, J. R., 64.

Code numbers in registration, 100.

Cohen, J. L., 5, 20.

Cole, G. D. H., 43.

Compulsory insurance, employments excepted by Act of 1920, 171–73; opposition depends on agency exercising, 48, 157.

Contributions, collection of, 15; extent of under unemployment insurance Acts, 90–91; highest when unemployment worst, 149.

Court of Referees, 14, 36, 100, 104.

Cox, Harold, 108.

Demarcation question, 23–24, 156.

Dependants Grants (*see also*, Unemployed Workers' Dependants

Act), under O.W.D., 30; effect in checking insolvency of fund, 59.

Distress Committees, 4, 7.

Doles, probably less costly than insurance, 96.

Dual relief, due to low benefits, 146; in Birmingham, 80; results of, 148; under Act of 1911, 79; under Act of 1920, 79; under Act of 1922 (April), 80.

Economic justification of unemployment insurance, 88 *et seq.*

Employment exchanges, attempted use of, to break trade-union standards, 114; burden of unemployment insurance upon, 123 *et seq.*; compulsory notification of vacancies to, 112–13; decline of vacancies notified, 118; defects of premises, 110–11; denied a fair chance by unemployment insurance, 145; efficiency during post-war depression, 118–19, 121; established as national system, 7; established as preliminary to insurance, 8, 115; failure of well-organized trades to utilize, 109–10; fundamental purpose of, 9, 88; neutrality in strikes and lockouts, 114; obstacle of newspaper advertising to, 112; overtime worked in, 124; press attacks on, 108; routine work of, 99 *et seq.*; services rendered by, 144; size of personnel, 120 *et seq.*; State should operate, 149; statistical work of (summarized), 141–43; statistics of placing work, 116; Tavistock Street Exchange, 110; unable to regularize demand for labor, 144; vacancies filled by, 120; vacancy sections of, 104.

Exemption certificates, 35.

Export Credits Scheme, 150, 189.

Fraudulent claiming, 146.

# LIST OF STUDIES IN ECONOMICS AND POLITICAL SCIENCE.

*Series of Monographs by Lecturers and Students connected with the London School of Economics and Political Science.*

EDITED BY THE

DIRECTOR OF THE LONDON SCHOOL OF ECONOMICS AND POLITICAL SCIENCE.

**1. The History of Local Rates in England.** The substance of five lectures given at the School in November and December, 1895. By EDWIN CANNAN, M.A., LL.D. 1896; second enlarged edition, 1912; xv. and 215 pp., Crown 8vo, cloth. 4s. net.
*P. S. King & Son.*

**2. Select Documents Illustrating the History of Trade Unionism.** I.—THE TAILORING TRADE. By F. W. GALTON. With a Preface by SIDNEY WEBB, LL.B. 1896; 242 pp., Crown 8vo cloth. 5s.
*P. S King & Son.*

**3. German Social Democracy.** Six lectures delivered at the School in February and March, 1896. By the HON. BERTRAND RUSSELL, B.A., late Fellow of Trinity College, Cambridge. With an Appendix on Social Democracy and the Woman Question in Germany. By ALYS RUSSELL, B.A. 1896: 204 pp., Crown 8vo, cloth. 3s. 6d.
*P. S. King & Son.*

**4. The Referendum in Switzerland.** By M SIMON DEPLOIGE, University of Louvain. With a Letter on the Referendum in Belgium by M. J. VAN DEN HEUVEL, Professor of International Law in the University of Louvain. Translated by C. P. TREVELYAN, M.A., Trinity College, Cambridge, and edited with Notes, Introduction, Bibliography, and Appendices by LILIAN TOMN (Mrs. Knowles), of Girton College, Cambridge, Research Student at the School. 1898; x. and 334 pp., Cr. 8vo, cloth. 7s. 6d. *P. S. King & Son.*

**5. The Economic Policy of Colbert.** By A. J. SARGENT, M.A., Senior Hulme Exhibitioner, Brasenose College, Oxford; and Whately Prizeman, 1897, Trinity College Dublin. 1899; viii. and 138 pp., Crown 8vo, cloth. 2s. 6d. *P. S. King & Son.*

**6. Local Variations in Wages** (The Adam Smith Prize, Cambridge University, 1898). By F. W. LAWRENCE, M.A., Fellow of Trinity College, Cambridge. 1899; viii. and 90 pp., with Index and 18 Maps and Diagrams. Quarto, 11 in. by 8½ in., cloth. 8s. 6d.
*Longmans, Green & Co.*

**7. The Receipt Roll of the Exchequer for Michaelmas Term of the Thirty-first Year of Henry II. (1185).** A unique fragment transcribed and edited by the Class in Palæography and Diplomatic, under the supervision of the Lecturer, HUBERT HALL. F.S.A., of H.M. Public Record Office. With thirty-one Facsimile Plates in Collotype and Parallel readings from the contemporary Pipe Roll. 1899; vii. and 37 pp., Folio, 15½ in. by 11½ in., in green cloth; 2 Copies left. Apply to the Director of the London School of Economics.

## LIST OF STUDIES.

**8. Elements of Statistics.** By ARTHUR L. BOWLEY, M.A., Sc.D., F.S.S., Cobden and Adam Smith Prizeman, Cambridge; Guy Silver Medallist of the Royal Statistical Society; Newmarch Lecturer, 1897—8. 500 pp. and 40 Diagrams, Demy 8vo, cloth. 1901; Third edition, 1907; viii. and 336 pp. 12s. net.

*P. S. King & Son.*

**9. The Place of Compensation in Temperance Reform.** By C. P. SANGER, M.A., late Fellow of Trinity College, Cambridge, Barrister-at-Law. 1901; viii. and 136 pp., Crown 8vo, cloth. 2s. 6d net.

*P. S. King & Son.*

**10. A History of Factory Legislation.** By B. L. HUTCHINS and A. HARRISON (Mrs. Spencer), B.A., D.Sc. (Econ.), London. With a Preface by SIDNEY WEBB, LL.B. 1903; new and revised edition, 1911; xvi. and 298 pp., Demy 8vo, cloth. 7s. 6d. net.

*P. S. King & Son.*

**11. The Pipe Roll of the Exchequer of the See of Winchester for the Fourth Year of the Episcopate of Peter des Roches (1207).** Transcribed and edited from the original Roll in the possession of the Ecclesiastical Commissioners by the Class in Palæography and Diplomatic, under the supervision of the Lecturer, HUBERT HALL, F.S.A., of H.M. Public Record Office. With a Frontispiece giving a Facsimile of the Roll. 1903; xlviii. and 100 pp., Folio, 13¼ in. by 8½ in., green cloth. 15s. net

*P. S. King & Son.*

**12. Self-Government in Canada and How it was Achieved : The Story of Lord Durham's Report.** By F. BRADSHAW, B.A., D.Sc. (Econ.), London; Senior Hulme Exhibitioner, Brasenose College, Oxford. 1903; 414 pp., Demy 8vo, cloth. 7s. 6d. net.

*P. S. King & Son.*

**13. History of the Commercial and Financial Relations Between England and Ireland from the Period of the Restoration.** By ALICE EFFIE MURRAY (Mrs. Radice), D.Sc. (Econ.), London, former Student at Girton College, Cambridge; Research Student of the London School of Economics and Political Science. 1903; 486 pp., Demy 8vo, cloth. 7s. 6d. net.

*P. S. King & Son.*

**14. The English Peasantry and the Enclosure of Common Fields.** By GILBERT SLATER, M.A., St. John's College, Cambridge; D.Sc. (Econ.), London. 1906; 337 pp., Demy 8vo, cloth. 10s. 6d. net.

*Constable & Co.*

**15. A History of the English Agricultural Labourer.** By Dr. W. HASBACH, Professor of Economics in the University of Kiel. Translated from the Second Edition (1908), by Ruth Kenyon. Introduction by SIDNEY WEBB, LL.B. 1908; xvi. and 470 pp., Demy 8vo, cloth. 7s. 6d. net.

*P. S. King & Son.*

**16. A Colonial Autocracy : New South Wales under Governor Macquarie, 1810-21.** By MARION PHILLIPS, B.A., Melbourne; D.Sc. (Econ.), London. 1909; xxiii. and 336 pp., Demy 8vo, cloth. 10s. 6d. net.

*P. S. King & Son.*

# LIST OF STUDIES.

**17. India and the Tariff Problem.** By H. B. LEES SMITH, M.A. M.P. 1909 ; 120 pp., Crown 8vo, cloth. 3s. 6d. net.

*Constable & Co.*

**18. Practical Notes on the Management of Elections.** Three Lectures delivered at the School in November, 1909, by ELLIS T. POWELL, LL.B., D.Sc. (Econ.), London, Fellow of the Royal Historical and Royal Economic Societies, of the Inner Temple, Barrister-at-Law. 1909 ; 52 pp., 8vo, paper. 1s. 6d. net.

*P. S. King & Son.*

**19. The Political Development of Japan.** By G. E. UYEHARA, B.A., Washington, D.Sc. (Econ.), London. xxiv. and 296 pp., Demy 8vo, cloth. 1910. 8s. 6d. net. *Constable & Co.*

**20. National and Local Finance.** By J. WATSON GRICE, D.Sc. (Econ.), London. Preface by SIDNEY WEBB, LL.B. 1910 ; 428 pp., Demy 8vo, cloth. 12s. net. *P. S. King & Son.*

**21. An Example of Communal Currency.** Facts about the Guernsey Market-house. By J. THEODORE HARRIS, B.A., with an Introduction by SIDNEY WEBB, LL.B. 1911 ; xiv. and 62 pp., Crown 8vo, cloth. 1s. 6d. net ; paper, 1s. net. *P. S. King & Son.*

**22. Municipal Origins.** History of Private Bill Legislation. By F. H. SPENCER, LL.B., D.Sc. (Econ.), London ; with a Preface by Sir EDWARD CLARKE, K.C. 1911 ; xi. and 333 pp., Demy 8vo, cloth. 10s. 6d. net. *Constable & Co.*

**23. Seasonal Trades.** By VARIOUS AUTHORS. With an Introduction by SIDNEY WEBB. Edited by SIDNEY WEBB, LL.B., and ARNOLD FREEMAN, M.A. 1912 ; xi. and 410 pp., Demy 8vo, cloth. 7s. 6d. net. *Constable & Co.*

**24. Grants in Aid.** A Criticism and a Proposal. By SIDNEY WEBB, LL.B. 1911 ; vii. and 135 pp., Demy 8vo, cloth. 5s. net.

*Longmans, Green & Co.*

**25. The Panama Canal : A Study in International Law.** By H. ARIAS, B.A., LL.D. 1911 ; xiv. and 188 pp., 2 maps, bibliography, Demy 8vo, cloth. 10s. 6d. net. *P. S. King & Son.*

**26. Combination Among Railway Companies.** By W. A. ROBERTSON, B.A. 1912 ; 105 pp., Demy 8vo, cloth. 1s. 6d. net ; paper, 1s. net. *Constable & Co.*

**27. War and the Private Citizen : Studies in International Law.** By A. PEARCE HIGGINS, M.A., LL.D. ; with Introductory Note by the Rt. Hon. Arthur Cohen, K.C. 1912 ; xvi. and 200 pp., Demy 8vo, cloth. 5s. net. *P. S. King & Son.*

**28. Life in an English Village :** An Economic and Historical Survey of the Parish of Corsley, in Wiltshire. By M. F. DAVIES. 1909 ; xiii. and 319 pp., illustrations, bibliography, Demy 8vo, cloth, 10s. 6d. net. *T. Fisher Unwin.*

# LIST OF STUDIES.

**29. English Apprenticeship and Child Labour : A History.** By O. JOCELYN DUNLOP, D.Sc. (Econ.), London ; with a Supplementary Section on the Modern Problem of Juvenile Labour, by the Author and R. D. DENMAN, M.P. 1912 ; 390 pp., bibliography, Demy 8vo, cloth. 10s. 6d. net. *T. Fisher Unwin.*

**30. Origin of Property and the Formation of the Village Community.** By J. ST. LEWINSKI, D.Ec.Sc., Brussels. 1913 ; xi. and 71 pp., Demy 8vo, cloth. 3s. 6d. net. *Constable & Co.*

**31. The Tendency towards Industrial Combination (in some Spheres of British Industry).** By G. R. CARTER, M.A. 1913 ; xxiii. and 391 pp., Demy 8vo, cloth. 6s. net. *Constable & Co.*

**32. Tariffs at Work :** An Outline of Practical Tariff Administration. By JOHN HEDLEY HIGGINSON, B.Sc.(Econ.), London, Mitchel-Student of the University of London ; Cobden Prizeman and Silver Medallist. 1913 ; 150 pp., Crown 8vo, cloth. 2s. 6d. net. *P. S. King & Son.*

**33. English Taxation, 1640-1799.** An Essay on Policy and Opinion. By WILLIAM KENNEDY, M.A., D.Sc. (Econ.), London ; Shaw Research Student of the London School of Economics and Political Science. 1913 ; 200 pp., Demy 8vo. 7s. 6d. net. *G. Bell & Sons.*

**34. Emigration from the United Kingdom to North America, 1763-1912.** By STANLEY C. JOHNSON, M.A., Cambridge, D.Sc. (Econ.), London. 1913 ; xvi. and 387 pp., Demy 8vo, cloth. 6s. net. *G. Routledge & Sons.*

**35. The Financing of the Hundred Years' War, 1337-60.** By SCHUYLER B. TERRY. 1913 ; xvi. and 199 pp., Demy 8vo, cloth. 6s. net. *Constable & Co.*

**36. Kinship and Social Organization.** By W. H. R. RIVERS, M.D., F.R.S., Fellow of St. John's College, Cambridge. 1914 ; 96 pp., Demy 8vo, cloth. 2s. 6d. net. *Constable & Co.*

**37. The Nature and First Principle of Taxation.** By ROBERT JONES, D.Sc. (Econ.), London ; with a Preface by SIDNEY WEBB, LL.B. 1914 ; xvii. and 299 pp., Demy 8vo, cloth. 7s. 6d. net. *P. S. King & Son.*

**38. The Export of Capital.** By C. K. HOBSON, M.A., D.Sc. (Econ.), London, F.S.S., Shaw Research Student of the London School of Economics and Political Science. 1914 ; xxv. and 264 pp., Demy 8vo, cloth. 7s. 6d. net. *Constable & Co.*

**39. Industrial Training.** By NORMAN BURRELL DEARLE, M.A., D.Sc. (Econ.), London, Fellow of All Souls College, Oxford ; Shaw Research Student of the London School of Economics and Political Science. 1914 ; 610 pp., Demy 8vo. cloth. 10s. 6d. net. *P. S. King & Son.*

# LIST OF STUDIES.

**40. Theory of Rates and Fares.** From the French of Charles Colson's " Transports et tarifs " (3rd edn., 1907), by L. R. CHRISTIE, G. LEEDHAM and C. TRAVIS. Edited and arranged by CHARLES TRAVIS, with an Introduction by W. M. ACWORTH, M.A. 1914 ; viii. and 195 pp., Demy 8vo, cloth. 3s. 6d. net. *G. Bell & Sons, Ltd.*

**41. Advertising : A Study of a Modern Business Power.** By G. W. GOODALL, B.Sc. (Econ.), London ; with an Introduction by SIDNEY WEBB, LL.B. 1914 ; xviii. and 91 pp., Demy 8vo, cloth. 2s. 6d. net ; paper, 1s. 6d. net. *Constable & Co.*

**42. English Railways : Their Development and their Relation to the State.** By EDWARD CARNEGIE CLEVELAND-STEVENS, M.A., Christ Church, Oxford ; D.Sc. (Econ.), London ; Shaw Research Student of the London School of Economics and Political Science. 1915 ; xvi. and 325 pp., Demy 8vo, cloth. 6s. net. *G. Routledge & Sons.*

**43. The Lands of the Scottish Kings in England.** By MARGARET F. MOORE, M.A., ; with an Introduction by P. HUME BROWN, M.A., LL.D., D.D., Professor of Ancient Scottish History and Palæography, University of Edinburgh. 1915 ; xii. and 141 pp., Demy 8vo, cloth. 5s. net. *George Allen & Unwin.*

**44. The Colonization of Australia, 1829-42 : The Wakefield Experiment in Empire Building.** By RICHARD C. MILLS, LL.M., Melbourne ; D.Sc. (Econ.), London ; with an Introduction by GRAHAM WALLAS, M.A., Professor of Political Science in the University of London. 1915 ; xx., 363 pp., Demy 8vo, cloth. 10s. 6d. net.
*Sidgwick & Jackson.*

**45. The Philosophy of Nietzsche.** By A. WOLF, M.A., D.Lit., Fellow of University College, London ; Reader in Logic and Ethics in the University of London. 1915 ; 114 pp., Demy 8vo, cloth. 3s. 6d. net. *Constable & Co.*

**46. English Public Health Administration.** By B. G. BANNINGTON ; with a Preface by GRAHAM WALLAS, M.A., Professor of Political Science in the University of London. 1915 ; xiv., 338 pp., Demy 8vo, cloth. 8s. 6d. net. *P. S. King & Son.*

**47. British Incomes and Property : The Application of Official Statistics to Economic Problems.** By J. C. STAMP D.Sc. (Econ.), London. 1916 ; xvi., 538 pp., Demy 8vo, cloth. 12s. 6d. net.
*P. S. King & Son.*

**48. Village Government in British India.** By JOHN MATTHAI, D.Sc. (Econ.), London ; with a Preface by SIDNEY WEBB, LL.B., Professor of Public Administration in the University of London. 1915 ; xix., 211 pp., Demy 8vo, cloth. 4s. 6d. net.
*T. Fisher Unwin.*

**49. Welfare Work : Employers' Experiments for Improving Working Conditions in Factories.** By E. D. PROUD (Mrs. Gordon Pavy), B.A., Adelaide ; D.Sc. (Econ.), London ; with a Foreword by the Rt. Hon. D. Lloyd George, M.P., Prime Minister. 1916 ; 3rd edn., 1918 ; xx., 368 pp., Demy 8vo, cloth. 8s. 6d. net.
*George Bell & Sons.*

# LIST OF STUDIES.

**50. The Development of Rates of Postage.** By A. D. SMITH, D.Sc. (Econ.), London, F.S.S., of the Secretary's Office, General Post Office ; with an Introduction by the Rt. Hon. HERBERT SAMUEL, M.P., Postmaster-General, 1910-4 and 1915-6. 1917 ; xii., 431 pp. Demy 8vo, cloth. 16s. net. *George Allen & Unwin.*

**51. Metaphysical Theory of the State.** By L. T. HOBHOUSE, M.A., Martin White Professor of Sociology in the University of London. 1918 ; 156 pp., Demy 8vo, cloth. 7s. 6d. net.
*George Allen & Unwin.*

**52. Outlines of Social Philosophy.** By J. S. MACKENZIE, M.A., Professor of Logic and Philosophy in the University College of South Wales. 1918 ; 280 pp., Demy 8vo, cloth. 10s. 6d. net.
*George Allen & Unwin.*

**53. Economic Phenomena Before and After War.** By SLAVKO SECEROV, Ph.D., M.Sc. (Econ.), London, F.S.S. 1919 ; viii., 226 pp., Demy 8vo, cloth. 10s. 6d. net. *G. Routledge & Sons.*

**54. Gold, Prices, and the Witwatersrand.** By R. A. LEHFELDT, D.Sc., Professor of Economics at the South African School of Mines and Technology, Johannesburg (University of South Africa) ; Correspondent for South Africa of the Royal Economic Society. 1919 ; 130 pp., Crown 8vo, cloth. 5s. net. *P. S. King & Son.*

**55. Exercises in Logic.** By A. WOLF, M.A., D.Lit., Fellow of University College, London ; Reader in Logic and Ethics in the University of London. 1919 ; 78 pp., Crown 8vo, paper. 3s. net.
*George Allen & Unwin.*

**56. Working Life of Women in the 17th Century.** By ALICE CLARK, Shaw Research Student of the London School of Economics and Political Science. 1919 ; (7), 335 pp., Demy 8vo, cloth. 10s. 6d. net. *G. Routledge & Sons.*

**57. Animal Foodstuffs : With Special Reference to the British Empire and the Food Supply of the United Kingdom.** By E. W. SHANAHAN, M.A., New Zealand ; D.Sc. (Econ.), London. 1920 ; viii., 331 pp., Demy 8vo, cloth. 10s. 6d. net. *G. Routledge & Sons.*

**58. Commercial Advertising.** A course of lectures given at the School. By THOMAS RUSSELL, President of the Incorporated Society of Advertisement Consultants ; sometime Advertisement Manager of the *Times.* 1919 ; x., 306 pp., Demy 8vo, cloth. 10s. 6d. net.
*G. P. Putnam's Sons.*

**59. Some Aspects of The Inequality of Incomes in Modern Communities.** By HUGH DALTON, M.A., King's College, Cambridge ; Barrister-at-Law of the Middle Temple ; Hutchinson Research Student of the London School of Economics and Political Science. 1920 ; xii. and 360 pp., Demy 8vo, cloth. 10s. 6d. net. *G. Routledge & Sons.*

**60. History of Social Development.** From the German of F. Müller-Lyer's " Phasen der Kultur," 1908, by E. C. and H. A. LAKE.
*George Allen & Unwin.*

## LIST OF STUDIES.

**61.—The Industrial and Commercial Revolutions in Great Britain during the Nineteenth Century.**

By LILIAN C. A. KNOWLES, Litt.D., Dublin; Hist. Tripos and Law Tripos. Girton College, Cambridge ; Reader in Economic History in the University of London. 1921 ; xii. and 412 pp., Crown 8vo, Cloth. 6s. 6d. net. *G. Routledge & Sons.*

**62.—Tariffs : a Study in Method.**

By T. E. G. GREGORY, B.Sc. (Econ.), London ; Sir Ernest Cassel Reader in Commerce in the University of London. 1921 ; xv. and 518 pp., Demy 8vo, Cloth. 25s. net. *Charles Griffin & Co.*

**63.—The Theory of Marginal Value.**

Nine Lectures delivered at the School in Michaelmas Term, 1920. By L. V. BIRCK, M.A., D.Ec. Sc., Professor of Economics and Finance in the University of Copenhagen. 1922 ; viii. and 351 pp., Demy 8vo, Cloth. 14s. net. *G. Routledge & Sons.*

**64.—The Principle of Official Independence.**

By R. MCGREGOR DAWSON, M.Sc. (Econ.) London., M.A. [in the Press]. *P. S. King & Son.*

**65.—Argonauts of the Western Pacific.**

An Account of Native Enterprise and Adventure in the Archipelagoes of Eastern New Guinea. By BRONISLAW MALINOWSKI, Ph.D. (Cracow). D.Sc. (Lond.), ROBERT MOND Travelling Scholar (Univ. of Lond.). *G. Routledge & Sons.*

**66.—The First Principles of Public Finance.**

By HUGH DALTON, M.A., King's College, Cambridge. *G. Routledge & Sons*

# LIST OF STUDIES.

*Monographs on Sociology.*

**3. The Material Culture and Social Institutions of the Simpler Peoples.** By L. T. HOBHOUSE, M.A., Martin White Professor of Sociology in the University of London, G. C. WHEELER, B.A., and M. GINSBERG, B.A. 1915 ; 300 pp., Demy 8vo, paper. 2s. 6d. net.
*Chapman & Hall.*

**4. Village and Town Life in China.** By TAO LI KUNG, B.Sc. (Econ.), London, and LEONG YEW KOH, LL.B., B.Sc. (Econ.), London. Edited by L. T. HOBHOUSE, M.A. 1915 ; 153 pp., Demy 8vo, cloth. 5s. net.
*George Allen & Unwin.*

*Series of Bibliographies by Students of the School.*

**1. A Bibliography of Unemployment and the Unemployed.** By F. ISABEL TAYLOR, B.Sc. (Econ.), London. Preface by SIDNEY WEBB, LL.B. 1909 ; xix. and 71 pp., Demy 8vo, cloth, 2s. net ; paper, 1s. 6d. net.
*P. S. King & Son.*

**2. Two Select Bibliographies of Mediæval Historical Study.** By MARGARET F. MOORE, M.A. ; with Preface and Appendix by HUBERT HALL, F.S.A. 1912 ; 185 pp., Demy 8vo, cloth. 5s. net.
*Constable & Co.*

**3. Bibliography of Roadmaking and Roads in the United Kingdom.** By DOROTHY BALLEN, B.Sc. (Econ.), London : an enlarged and revised edition of a similar work compiled by Mr. and Mrs. Sidney Webb in 1906. 1914 ; xviii. and 281 pp., Demy 8vo, cloth. 15s. net.
*P. S. King & Son.*

**4. A Select Bibliography for the Study, Sources, and Literature of English Mediæval Economic History.** Edited by HUBERT HALL, F.S.A. 1914 ; xiii. and 350 pp., Demy 8vo, cloth. 5s. net.
*P. S. King & Son.*

*Series of Geographical Studies.*

**1. The Reigate Sheet of the One-Inch Ordnance Survey.** A Study in the Geography of the Surrey Hills. By ELLEN SMITH. Introduction by H. J. MACKINDER, M.A., M.P. 1910 ; xix. and 110 pp., 6 maps, 23 illustrations. Crown 8vo, cloth. 5s. net.
*A. & C. Black.*

**2. The Highlands of South-West Surrey.** A Geographical Study in Sand and Clay. By E. C. MATTHEWS. 1911 ; viii. and 124 pp., 7 maps, 8 illustrations, 8vo, cloth. 5s. net. *A. & C. Black.*

*Series of Contour Maps of Critical Areas.*

**1. The Hudson-Mohawk Gap.** Prepared by the Diagram Company from a map by B. B Dickinson. 1913 ; 1 sheet 18 in. by 22½in. Scale 20 miles to 1 inch. 6d. net ; post free, folded 7d., rolled 9d.
*Sifton, Praed & Co.*

# LIST OF STUDIES.

### 67.—Commercial Relations between England and India.

By BAL KRISHNA, Ph.D. (Econ.), London, M.A., F.S.S.; Principal, Rajaram College, Kolhapur, Bombay. *G. Routledge & Sons.*

### 68.—Wages in the Coal Industry.

By J. W. F. ROWE, B.A., Cambridge. 1923; (viii.) 174 pp., Demy 8vo, 10s. 6d. net. *P. S. King & Sons*

### 69.—The Co-operative Movement in Japan.

By KIYOSHI OGATA, B.Com., Tokyo. Preface by Professor SIDNEY WEBB, LL.B., M.P. 1923; xv., 362 pp., Demy 8vo, cloth. 12s. 6d. net. *P. S. King & Son.*

### 70.—The British Trade Boards System.

By DOROTHY SELLS, M.A., Ph.D. 1923; vii, 293 pp., Demy 8vo, cloth. 12s. 6d. net. *P. S. King & Son.*

### 71.—Second chambers in Theory and Practice.

By H. B. LEES-SMITH, M.A. 1923; 256 pp., Demy 8vo, cloth. 7s. 6d. net. *George Allen and Unwin.*

### 72.—Chinese Coolie Emigration to Countries within the British Empire.

By PERSIA CRAWFORD CAMPBELL, M.A. (Sydney); M.Sc. (Econ ), London; British Fellow of Bryn Mawr College, U.S.A., 1922-23. Preface by Hon. W. PEMBER REEVES, Ph.D. 1923; xxiii., 240 pp., Demy 8vo, cloth. 10s. 6d. net. *P. S. King & Son.*

### 73.—The rôle of the State in the provision of Railways.

By H. M. JAGTIANI, M.Sc. (Econ.), London, Barrister-at-Law; B.A., LL.B., Bombay. Introduction by Sir WILLIAM ACKWORTH, K.C.S.I. 1924; xi, 146 pp., Demy 8vo, cloth. 8s. 6d. net. *P. S. King & Son.*

### 74.—Dock Labour and Decasualisation.

By E. C. P. LASCELLES and S. S. BULLOCK, *Ratan Tata* Research Student, London School of Economics. 1924; xi, 201 pp., Demy 8vo, cloth. 10s. 6d. net. *P. S. King & Son.*

### 75.—Labour and Housing in Bombay.

By A. R. BURNETT-HURST, M.Sc. (Econ.), London; Professor, and Dean of the Faculties, of Commerce and Economics, University of Allahabad. [In the Press.] *P. S. King & Son.*

### 76.—The Economic Development of the British Overseas Empire since the acquisition of Canada.

By L. C. A. KNOWLES, M.A., Litt.D., Trinity Coll., Dublin; Lecturer at the London School of Economics. Demy 8vo. cloth. 10s. 6d. net. *G. Routledge & Sons, Ltd.*

### 77.—Unemployment Relief in Great Britain : a study in State Socialism.

By FELIX MORLEY. 1924; xvii and 204 pp, Large Crown 8vo, cloth, 6s. net. *G. Routledge & Sons.*

# LIST OF STUDIES

*Series of Geographical Studies.*

**3.—London on the Thames : a Geographical Study.** By (Mrs )
HILDA ORMSBY, B.Sc. (Econ.), London. 1924 ; xiv, 190 pp., maps, ills..
Demy 8vo, cloth. 8s. 6d. net. *Sifton, Praed & Co.*

*Series of Bibliographies.*

**5.—A Guide to British Parliamentary and Official Publications.**
By H. B. LEES-SMITH, M.A., Queen's College, Oxford ; Lecturer in
Public Administration in the London School of Economics. 1924 ;
23 pp., 4to, paper wrapper. 2s. net. *Oxford University Press.*

*Studies in Commerce.*

**1.—The True Basis of Efficiency.** By LAWRENCE R. DICKSEE,
M.Com., F.C.A. ; Sir Ernest Cassel Professor of Accountancy and Business
Methods in the University of London. 1922 ; xi, 90 pp., Demy 8vo.,
cloth. 5s. net. *Gee & Co.*

**2.—The Ship and her Work.** By Sir WESTCOTT STILE ABELL,
K.B.E., M.Eng., M.I.N.A., M.I.C.E. ; Chief Ship Surveyor, Lloyd's
Register of Shipping. 1923 ; 114 pp., iii diags., etc., 4 tabs., Demy 8vo,
cloth. 7s. 6d. net, *Gee & Co.*

For Product Safety Concerns and Information please contact our EU
representative  GPSR@taylorandfrancis.com
Taylor & Francis Verlag GmbH, Kaufingerstraße 24, 80331 München, Germany